NEVER GIVE UP

SMALL CHANGES

BIG

RESULTS

Your Guide to Personal Growth and Lasting Happiness

JAY NESBIT

Award-Winning Author of *Rise Above The Rut*

ONE BOOKS PUBLISHING, LLC
One University Circle – Suite 1402
Cleveland, OH 44106
onebookspublishing@gmail.com

Editing by: Elizabeth (Haley) Larkin
Cover and Interior Design by: B. Bookclaw (www.bookclaw.com)

Small Changes BIG RESULTS:
Your Guide to Personal Growth and Lasting Happiness

ISBN: 979-8-9884949-5-9 (hardcover)
ISBN: 979-8-9884949-7-3 (paperback)
ISBN: 979-8-9884949-6-6 (eBook)
Library of Congress Control Number: 2024911977

FIRST EDITION
www.jaynesbit.com

For my family and friends.

Thank you for joining me on this journey. Let's explore paths to growth and purpose together.

A FEW FACTS TO CONSIDER:

Did you know that making just a 1% improvement in your life every day can lead to a 365% improvement by the end of the year? It's all about the power of consistent, incremental changes adding up to significant transformations over time.

Research, from the Centers for Disease Control and Prevention (CDC), shows that even small lifestyle changes, like incorporating regular exercise or adopting healthier eating habits, can significantly reduce the risk of chronic diseases such as heart disease, diabetes, and certain cancers. Taking small steps toward a healthier lifestyle can lead to a longer, happier life.

Embracing new experiences, even in small doses, can broaden your perspective, boost your confidence, and enhance your overall well-being. Whether it's traveling to a new destination, learning a new hobby, or stepping out of your comfort zone, each small adventure contributes to your personal growth journey.

Making small improvements in your skills or professional network can open up new opportunities and propel your career forward. Whether it's learning a new software program, attending networking events, or seeking mentorship, each small step can bring you closer to your dream job or business venture.

History is filled with examples of individuals who faced countless setbacks and failures on their path to success. From Thomas Edison's numerous attempts before inventing the light bulb to J.K. Rowling's rejection letters before publishing Harry Potter, these stories remind us that perseverance in pursuing our dreams is key. Remember, every setback is an opportunity to learn and grow stronger.

HOW TO USE THIS BOOK FOR MAXIMUM IMPACT:

Thank you for picking up this book. You're about to start a journey of small habit changes that can lead to big transformations in your life. Before you dive into the chapters, let's talk about how you can make the most out of this book and really see lasting results.

1. Take Your Time. Don't rush through the chapters. Each one focuses on a different aspect of personal growth, and it's important to give yourself time to absorb and apply the ideas. You might find it helpful to spend a week or more on each chapter, trying out the exercises and reflecting on your experiences.

2. Keep an Open Mind. Some of the concepts might be new or seem challenging at first. That's totally okay! Approach each chapter with curiosity and a willingness to try something different. You might be surprised at how much you learn about yourself.

3. Reflect and Journal. Writing things down helps solidify your thoughts and track your progress. Use the journaling prompts at the end of each chapter to reflect on your experiences. This practice will help you see how far you've come and keep you motivated.

4. Be Consistent. Small changes add up over time. Consistency is key to seeing real benefits. Whether it's keeping a gratitude journal, practicing kindness, or nurturing optimism, make these practices a part of your daily routine.

5. Share Your Journey. Tell a friend or join a community that's focused on personal growth. Sharing your experiences can provide extra motivation and support. Plus, it's always great to have someone to celebrate your wins with!

6. Revisit and Reflect. Personal growth is an ongoing process. Revisit chapters periodically to see how your perspectives have evolved. Reflect on the progress you've made and identify areas where you can continue to grow.

7. Be Patient and Kind to Yourself. Habit change doesn't happen overnight. Be patient with yourself and recognize that setbacks are a part of the journey. Treat yourself with the same kindness and understanding you'd offer to a friend.

8. Apply What You Learn. This book is packed with practical tips and exercises. Make sure to put them into practice! Reading is just the first step—real change happens when you apply what you've learned to your daily life.

Why This Matters: The changes you'll read about aren't just feel-good ideas. They're backed by research and have been shown to improve happiness, resilience, and overall well-being. By following the guidance in this book, you're investing in a happier, healthier, and more fulfilling life.

So, grab your favorite journal, find a cozy spot, and let's get started on this journey together. Ready to make some small changes that lead to big results? Let's do this!

CONTENTS

INTRODUCTION

Life's quite the journey, isn't it? We've all felt that whirlwind, spinning us around until we're dizzy and disoriented, wondering where we're headed. But here's the scoop: *Small Changes BIG RESULTS* will guide you through the chaos and help you rediscover what really counts.

Finding the way forward: I've been in the trenches myself. Feeling trapped in the monotony of my lackluster pharmacy career and facing the uphill battle of a challenging divorce, I hit lows that made every day feel like a drag—no fun, no meaning, just a relentless sense of desolation.

But as those of you who've read my first book, *Rise Above the Rut,* know, I refused to stay stuck. I rolled up my sleeves and dove headfirst into figuring out why my life felt like an uphill battle and what I could do to improve it. I won't soften the truth for you—breaking ingrained habits takes effort and can be painful. But trust me, as we journey together, I'm confident you'll find growth, contentment, and purpose waiting for you.

Here's the kicker: It's all about the small changes. Sounds simple, right? Yet, it's the accumulation of those tiny tweaks that sets off monumental shifts, like crafting a skyscraper— one brick at a time. It demands grit, determination, and relentless effort, but believe me, every bit pays off.

Think about it: We've only got this one shot at life. There's no dress rehearsal; this is the real deal. With no guarantees on how long it'll last or how much time we have, why not make every moment count for the pursuit of happiness, meaning, and growth?

That's where *Small Changes BIG RESULTS* comes in. It's your roadmap to crafting a life that lights you up from the inside out. So, find your comfiest seat, grab a tall glass of water, and let's tackle this journey together. Every step we take brings us closer to a brighter, more fulfilling tomorrow. Are you ready to dive in? Awesome, let's do this!

***

YOUR ROADMAP TO SUCCESS: MASTERING THE 3-STEP PROCESS

It's super important to have a solid plan if you want to change or start new habits and actually stick with them. Here's the deal: most people fail at this. For example, around 90% of people who try to quit smoking relapse within a year (Lemmens, 2017). And about 50% of people who start a new exercise routine quit within the first six months (Marcus, 2019). But don't get discouraged. The key is having a plan that works.

That's where my *3-Step Plan* comes in. It's all about making small changes that add up to big results. Here's how it breaks down:

1. **Purpose:** First, take time for contemplation and figure out what you really want. What's the big goal that gets you excited? Knowing your "why" keeps you motivated. If you don't know or feel strongly about your purpose, you'll struggle to stay committed.

2. **Plan:** Next, map out a plan with clear, realistic goals. This makes your big dream feel real and doable. Break it down into smaller steps so it's not

overwhelming. Without an effective plan, it's easy to get lost and give up.

3. **Proceed:** Finally, take action with small, steady steps. It's all about keeping the momentum going. Even tiny progress is still progress. If you don't do the work needed to create a new healthy habit, you won't succeed.

In this book, you're about to dive into 15 small steps that lead to big results. But before you start, make sure you first read the chapter "Explaining the 3-Step Process" a couple of times. Get comfortable with the steps needed to reach your dream. This foundation is crucial for your success. By sticking to this method and following each step, you can make those small, important changes that lead to big, long-term success. It's simple, but it works!

Remember, every great journey begins with a single step.

NAVIGATING THE PATH TO GROWTH AND HAPPINESS

"Everyone wants to live on top of the mountain, but all the happiness and growth occurs while you're climbing it."

— ANDY ROONEY

Personal growth: It's about learning new skills, changing your mindset, and taking actions that make your life better overall.

Happiness: Feeling good about life, finding meaning in what you do, and being deeply content.

***

Picture this: you're standing at the foot of a mountain, gazing up at its towering peak. Your heart races with excitement at the thought of reaching the summit. But here's the truth: while the view from the top may be breathtaking, it's the journey of climbing that mountain where true happiness and growth unfold.

We all hope to be 'happy' and live a good life—whatever that means. Yet, what does happiness really entail? Happiness is tricky to define. The true meaning of happiness has been studied for centuries, and there are many definitions.

For our purposes, let's think of happiness, as described in modern psychology, as feeling good about our lives overall—a deep sense of contentment and fulfillment.

Happiness isn't solely achieved through the pursuit of pleasure; rather, it stems from striving toward goals that align with our values (Kesebir & Diener, 2008). These values are derived through understanding what brings genuine happiness, what holds true significance for us, and what aspirations we aim to fulfill. By dedicating ourselves to this ongoing journey, we not only gain a sense of purpose and fulfillment but also find meaning in our daily endeavors.

This book is part of my *Living with Purpose* series, which expands on the foundational principles laid out in my previous work, *Rise Above the Rut*, offering a 3-Step process for rediscovering joy and purpose in your life. The books in this series can be read and implemented in any order, allowing for a personalized journey to profound growth, change, and a sense of well-being.

As we venture into this exploration, keep in mind that the path to thriving isn't linear. It's a journey filled with twists and turns, ups and downs. However, each step forward, no matter how small, brings us closer to our destination—a life filled with genuine happiness and enjoyment, especially as we help each other along the way.

Striving for happiness is a big deal. It's not just about feeling good for a moment; it's about feeling genuinely content and fulfilled. That means finding joy in everyday stuff and keeping a positive mindset.

But how do we actually get there? Well, it's a mix of things like building strong relationships, doing stuff we love, and having a sense of purpose. It's about being true to ourselves and going after what really matters to us. And here's the thing—it's not like we just reach this happiness finish line. It's more like a never-ending journey of learning and growing.

And you know what? It's those small daily changes that really make the difference. Whether it's practicing gratitude, taking time for self-care, or doing something kind for someone else, every little bit adds up.

Plus, happiness isn't just a nice bonus. It's like fuel for our personal growth engine. When we're happy, whether we've nailed a goal or are doing something we adore, it gives us a boost. It pushes us to keep aiming high, tackle challenges, and dream big. Happiness isn't just a goal—it's our secret weapon for a kick-ass future.

Research in the fields of positive psychology and personal development has revealed that when we prioritize our life satisfaction, we unlock a myriad of benefits that extend far beyond momentary pleasure. Life satisfaction is like a superpower that enhances our resilience, motivation, and ability to form meaningful connections.

Throughout the following chapters of this book, we will explore fifteen *small changes* and how each of them contributes to our overall sense of happiness and well-being, ultimately leading us to thrive. From cultivating gratitude and practicing kindness to harnessing the power of visualization and learning confidence, each small change offers a unique pathway to enhancing our happiness and living a more fulfilling life.

These methods aren't about quick fixes or temporary pleasures; they're about making lasting changes that lead to a better overall quality of life.

Drawing on the latest research and expert insights, each technique outlined in this book provides invaluable guidance and practical steps supported by real-life examples and inspiring anecdotes.

Each chapter includes an inspiring quote, keyword definitions, suggestions for further learning, and journaling prompts to help you better understand and use the material to improve your life. These tools will serve as your companions on the journey to unlocking your full potential and creating a life that truly brings you joy and satisfaction.

Welcome to *Small Changes BIG RESULTS*, where we're not just aiming for the mountaintop—we're embracing the climb, the challenges, and the triumphs along the way. Just like all other living creatures, we either thrive or fade.

So, are you ready to move forward on a journey of self-discovery, empowerment, and fulfillment? Together, let's embrace the power of well-being and rise to new heights.

In the next chapter, we'll explore the practical *3-Step Process* outlined in my book *Rise Above the Rut*. This process will not only help you understand how change occurs but also what it takes to turn it into a lasting habit for a thriving life. For those of you already familiar with the 3-Step Process, feel free to skip the next chapter.

Following the chapter explaining the 3-Step Process, we will discuss how uncovering your passion and pursuing your purpose provide the groundwork for implementing the fifteen small steps ahead, ultimately enhancing your life.

EXPLAINING THE 3-STEP PROCESS

Note: I am including this chapter from my book, *Rise Above the Rut*, to provide you with additional guidance and inspiration. I believe that the insights shared in this chapter are valuable and relevant to implementing the 15 small changes we will cover in this book.

"The two most important days in life are the day you were born and the day you find out why."

- MARK TWAIN

Rut: A habit or routine that's become boring and unproductive but tough to break out of.

Authentic life: Living true to your own values, skills, and passions, no matter what pressures you face.

Meaningful life: Living with purpose, significance, fulfillment, and satisfaction.

***

The book *Rise Above the Rut* is your key to unlocking a world of endless possibilities and embracing the unique person you were truly meant to be. You will discover a powerful process that leads to a life overflowing with purpose and deep meaning. Prepare to find the life-changing answers to three important questions that we've all wondered about at some point:

- *"How did I end up where I am today?"*
- *"Is there more to life than what I'm experiencing right now?"*
- *"Who am I really, at my core?"*

The 3-Step Process of "Purpose, Plan, and Progress" is designed to be easily understandable and applicable to vital areas of your life, including career, self-care, financial independence, relationships, lifestyle choices, and more. However, I won't sugarcoat it; it does require effort and resilience on your part. By diligently following this process, you'll bridge the gap between your current situation and your desired destination. Get ready to unlock a renewed sense of joy and purpose in your life. Here's an explanation of what you can expect from each step:

Step 1: Uncover your unique purpose through self-reflection that reveals your true or authentic self. You will ask yourself questions like "Why do I think, feel and act the way I do?" "What do I like to do?" "What am I good at?" "What do I value in life?" Two helpful routes for effective reflection are acting mindful and journaling. Effective introspection allows you to understand your current situation better.

Completing Step 1 leads to you becoming fully aware of your purpose, also known as your "why." Your purpose is your central, motivating aim in life. It drives and energizes you and provides you with a sense of direction for everything you do. Knowing your purpose simplifies decision-making and goal-setting.

Step 2: Now that you have self-understanding, have identified your purpose, and know your starting point, you can visualize where you want to go and develop a plan to get there. You'll learn to choose large and small goals and action steps that all correspond with your purpose. Your plan will include making the best use of your time and energy.

You'll know if you have chosen the right goals because you will feel enjoyment as you pursue those goals in Step 3. Your days will feel interesting and meaningful. It will feel like what you are doing is what you were born to do.

Step 3: The final step is to show up and make progress. To make successful progress as you take action on your plan, you will want to acquire a toolkit full of knowledge, skills, and good habits. These essential personal qualities enable you to persist even in the face of mistakes and obstacles that arise on your chosen path. You'll learn to control unhelpful thoughts and emotions.

When it comes to accomplishing what truly matters to you, there are no magical shortcuts or quick fixes. None of us are born with the knowledge of how to live life to the absolute fullest.

It calls for an unwavering desire to initiate the journey, a steadfast commitment to continuous learning and evolution, and the remarkable courage to conquer fear and embrace risks.

But let me assure you, the reward is immeasurable: it's about unleashing a life that surpasses even your wildest dreams, filling each moment with authentic fulfillment and limitless joy. That's what it means to be true to yourself and live your best life.

I am genuinely excited to work with you on achieving your vision. However, it's important to acknowledge, once again, that reaching your full potential requires effort and dedication on your part. Together, we will embark on a life-changing journey that will shape the rewarding life you were meant to live.

IN A NUTSHELL:

Picture the life you want and know what you want to change. Start from where you are, using what you have. Make a plan and take action. Be patient and learn from any bumps along the way. Take good care of yourself and keep going strong.

CONTINUING EDUCATION RESOURCES:

1. *Finding Your Element: How to Discover Your Talents and Passions and Transform Your Life* by Ken Robinson
2. *The Gifts of Imperfection: Let Go of Who You Think You're Supposed to Be and Embrace Who You Are* by Brené Brown
3. *The Values Factor: The Secret to Creating an Inspired and Fulfilling Life* by Dr. John Demartini
4. *The Four Agreements: A Practical Guide to Personal Freedom* by Don Miguel
5. *The Happiness Advantage: How a Positive Brain Fuels Success in Work and Life* by Shawn Achor

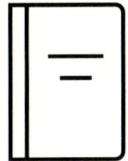

JOURNALING PROMPTS:

Journaling prompts are a great way to help you engage with the material and reflect on your own experiences. Here are two prompts for this chapter:

Journal Prompt 1: Reflect on a time when you felt stuck in a rut or uncertain about your future. What were the circumstances, and how did you navigate through that challenging period? What lessons did you learn from that experience, and how did it shape your perspective on pursuing your dreams?

Journal Prompt 2: Imagine yourself five years from now, living your ideal life filled with purpose and fulfillment. What does that life look like for you? What steps can you take today to move closer to that vision? Take some time to jot down specific goals and action plans to help you turn your dreams into reality.

UNCOVERING YOUR PASSION AND PURPOSE

"If you have a strong purpose in life, you don't have to be pushed. Your passion will drive you there."

-   ROY T. BENNETT

Passion: That strong feeling or emotion that really drives you.

Purpose: Knowing what you want in life and having a clear path to get there.

***

Do you ever feel like you're just going through the motions, unsure of what really sets your soul on fire? You're not alone. Many of us find ourselves drifting aimlessly, searching for something that gives our lives meaning and purpose.

But fear not, because in this chapter, we're going to explore how to reconnect with your passions and discover your true calling. Understanding the importance of finding passion and pursuing purpose lays the foundation for the methods ahead, as they are designed to align with your authentic desires and aspirations, ultimately leading to a more fulfilling and satisfying life journey.

REDISCOVERING YOUR PASSIONS:

Think back to when you were a kid. Remember the things that made you light up with excitement? Maybe it was painting colorful pictures, strumming on a guitar, or exploring the great outdoors. Those moments of joy and wonder are still inside you, waiting to be rediscovered. Take some time to reflect on those childhood passions and consider how you can bring them back into your life today.

For example, Sarah used to find immense joy in creating stories and sharing them with her friends. However, as she grew older, the responsibilities of adulthood overshadowed her passion for storytelling. One day, she stumbled upon a local writing group and decided to give it a try.

As she sat down with pen in hand, a rush of excitement flooded back to her. The familiar act of putting words to paper brought back memories of her youth, where the magic of storytelling filled her with happiness. With each word she wrote, a sense of fulfillment washed over her, as if she had finally rediscovered a long-lost skill buried deep within her mind.

Sharing her stories with the writing group fueled her determination to pursue her passion wholeheartedly. Sarah's journey back to storytelling not only brought her immense happiness but also inspired her to embrace all the things that made her come alive. She realized that no matter how long she had been away from her childhood dreams, it was never too late to reignite that spark and pursue what truly mattered to her.

EXPLORING NEW INTERESTS:

Don't be afraid to step out of your comfort zone and try something new. Whether it's joining a pottery class, volunteering at an animal shelter, or learning a new language, exploring new interests can open doors to unexpected passions and opportunities. You never know what hidden talents and passions you might discover along the way.

For instance, take James. He'd always been curious about photography but never found the time to give it a try. One day, he decided to prioritize his interest and signed up for a photography workshop in his community. As he held the camera in his hands, he felt a surge of excitement and anticipation. With each click of the shutter, he found himself immersed in a world of creativity and expression he had never known before.

To his surprise, James fell deeply in love with capturing the beauty of the world through his camera lens. The way the sunlight danced through the trees, the candid smiles of strangers on the street – each moment frozen in time brought him immense joy and satisfaction. Photography became not only a hobby but also a source of purpose and fulfillment in his life.

With every photo he took, James felt a sense of connection to the world around him. In embracing his curiosity and taking that leap into the unknown, James opened up a world of possibilities and found true fulfillment in pursuing his passion for photography.

ALIGNING WITH YOUR VALUES:

Passion and purpose are closely tied to our values – the things that matter most to us in life. Take some time to clarify your values and consider how you can align your passions with them. For example, if one of your core values is environmental sustainability, you might find purpose in volunteering for a local conservation organization or starting a community garden.

Amy discovered her passion for environmental activism after learning about the impact of plastic pollution on marine life. She started volunteering with a local beach cleanup group and advocating for policies to reduce single-use plastics in her community. By aligning her passion for environmental sustainability with her values, Amy found a sense of purpose and fulfillment in making a positive difference in the world.

Amy's heart pounded with excitement as she joined her first beach cleanup event. With each piece of litter she picked up, she felt a deep sense of connection to the environment and a fierce determination to protect it. The sight of seabirds tangled in plastic debris fueled her passion for change, igniting a fire within her to advocate for policies that would safeguard our oceans and marine life. As she worked tirelessly to raise awareness about the dangers of plastic pollution, Amy found herself driven by a sense of purpose unlike anything she had experienced before. Every moment spent fighting for environmental sustainability reaffirmed her commitment to making a lasting impact on the world around her.

PURSUING YOUR PURPOSE:

Once you've identified your passions and aligned them with your values, it's time to start pursuing your purpose. This might mean making some bold choices or taking calculated risks, but trust me, it'll be worth it in the end. Whether it's starting a business, changing careers, or embarking on a new creative project, following your purpose will bring a sense of fulfillment and satisfaction that can't be matched by anything else.

Sarah, James, and Amy are just a few examples of people who have found passion and purpose in their lives by reconnecting with their interests, aligning them with their values, and pursuing their dreams. Remember, your passions are unique to you, and your purpose is waiting to be discovered. So, embrace the journey, follow your heart, and let your passions guide you toward a life filled with meaning and fulfillment.

As you finish up this chapter on finding what you love and what drives you, keep this in mind: the biggest satisfaction in life often comes from doing things that really matter to you. Enjoy the journey of getting to know yourself better because that's how you unlock your true potential. Each little step you take toward living authentically and going after what excites you brings you closer to making your dreams real.

Now, armed with newfound clarity and determination, let's dig into the 15 minor adjustments that will pave the way for your transformation—small changes with the power to create BIG RESULTS in your life.

CONTINUING EDUCATION RESOURCES TO UNCOVER YOUR PASSION AND PURPOSE:

1. *Finding Your Element: How to Discover Your Talents and Passions and Transform Your Life* by Ken Robinson
2. *Big Magic: Creative Living Beyond Fear* by Elizabeth Gilbert
3. *The Values Factor: The Secret to Creating an Inspired and Fulfilling Life* by Dr. John Demartini
4. *The Four Agreements: A Practical Guide to Personal Freedom* by Don Miguel Ruiz
5. *The Happiness Advantage: How a Positive Brain Fuels Success in Work and Life* by Shawn Achor

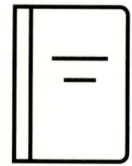

JOURNALING PROMPTS:

Journaling prompts are a great way to help you engage with the material and reflect on your own experiences. Here are two prompts to uncover your passion and purpose:

Journal Prompt 1: Reflect on a time when you felt truly alive and fulfilled, completely immersed in an activity or pursuit that resonated with your passions. What were you doing, and what made that experience so meaningful to you? Consider how you can incorporate more of those moments into your life today, and brainstorm actionable steps to reignite your sense of passion and purpose.

Journal Prompt 2: Imagine yourself five years from now, living a life that aligns perfectly with your passions and values. What does that life look like for you? Take some time to visualize your ideal future in vivid detail, from your career and relationships to your daily routines and overall sense of well-being. Then, reflect on what steps you can take today to start moving toward that vision, and commit to taking at least one concrete action toward your goals.

SMALL CHANGE 1:
CULTIVATING GRATITUDE

"Gratitude is thankfulness expressed in action."
-   WILLIAM GEORGE JORDAN

Gratitude: Feeling thankful and appreciative for the good things in your life.

***

So, you've been thinking about the purpose of your life, right? Well, here's something to keep that thought train rolling—gratitude. Have you ever felt like you're just going through the motions, like life is sort of happening to you without much excitement or direction? It's like you're on autopilot, not really feeling fully engaged or fulfilled.

But don't worry, because gratitude can change all of that. It's like adding color to a black-and-white movie. We're shifting gears from soul-searching to our first small change: gratitude. And trust me, it's a game-changer. So, get ready to explore how even a minor adjustment, like cultivating gratitude, can completely transform your perspective and bring more meaning into your life.

And here's the kicker: gratitude isn't just the beginning of our journey—it's the foundation for the 15 small changes we're about to dive into. Picture it like this: we're handing you a toolbox for life, and gratitude is the first tool we're placing in your hands. It's like laying down the groundwork for a solid house. So, without further ado, let's kick off this adventure by diving deep into the power of gratitude. Ready to improve your life? Let's do this!

UNDERSTANDING THE POWER OF GRATITUDE:

Gratitude is more than just saying "thank you" – it's a mindset, an attitude of appreciation and recognition for the good things in your life. It's about shifting your focus from what's lacking to what's present, from what's wrong to what's right.

Many studies in the fields of positive psychology, mental health, and well-being have demonstrated the positive effects of gratitude on various aspects of life (Emmons & McCullough, 2003; Wood et al., 2010; Seligman et al., 2005). Here's a summary of some key findings:

Increased Happiness and Life Satisfaction: Research has shown that individuals who regularly practice gratitude tend to experience higher levels of subjective well-being, happiness, and overall life satisfaction.

Improved Mental Health: Gratitude has been associated with reduced symptoms of depression and anxiety. Studies have shown that cultivating gratitude can lead to improvements in mood and emotional well-being.

Enhanced Resilience: Practicing gratitude has been linked to increased resilience, helping individuals cope with stress, trauma, and adversity more effectively.

Better Relationships: Expressing gratitude in relationships can strengthen social bonds, increase feelings of connection and intimacy, and foster a more positive relationship climate.

Physical Health Benefits: Some research suggests that gratitude may have positive effects on physical health as well. For example, gratitude practices have been associated with better sleep quality, reduced inflammation, and improved cardiovascular health.

So, what have we learned? Gratitude isn't just a feel-good concept; it's a powerhouse that can supercharge every aspect of your life. By embracing gratitude, you're not just saying thanks – you're opening the door to a happier, healthier, and more resilient you.

KEEPING A GRATITUDE JOURNAL:

One of the most effective ways to cultivate gratitude is by keeping a gratitude journal. This simple yet powerful practice involves regularly writing down things you're thankful for. By taking time each day to reflect on the bright spots in your life, you'll begin to notice a shift in your mindset and outlook.

Keeping a gratitude journal helps you become more attuned to the positive aspects of your life. It allows you to focus on what's going well rather than dwelling on what's not. Research has shown that people who keep gratitude journals experience greater levels of happiness, optimism, and life satisfaction (Wood et al., 2010; Diener and Tay, 2017).

One landmark study, conducted by psychologists Robert Emmons and Michael McCullough in 2003, found that participants who kept a gratitude journal for just three weeks experienced significant increases in happiness and overall well-being compared to those who did not. Other studies have shown that practicing gratitude can improve sleep quality, strengthen immune function, and enhance resilience in the face of adversity.

PRACTICAL TIPS FOR KEEPING A GRATITUDE JOURNAL:

To get started with your gratitude journal, set aside a few minutes each day to reflect on the things you're grateful for. It could be first thing in the morning, before you go to bed, or during a quiet moment in your day. Write down three things you're thankful for and take a moment to savor the feelings of gratitude that arise.

Make your gratitude journal a personalized reflection of your life. You can use a notebook, a digital journaling app, or even a gratitude jar where you can write down your gratitude on slips of paper. Get creative with your journaling practice—include drawings, photos, or quotes that inspire you. The key is to make it a habit and to be consistent in your practice.

And hey, since I'm all about personalizing here, why not take a moment to jot down what I'm grateful for today? Here's how I might write it in my journal:

Today, as I sit down to reflect on the good stuff in my life, I can't help but feel a surge of gratitude for the little joys that make each day special. First off, there's that heavenly scent of fresh coffee wafting through the air every morning, giving me a kickstart and getting me pumped for the day ahead. Then, there's the hearty laughter shared with a close friend over lunch, filling the air with warmth and bonding.

And let's not overlook the sheer delight of soaking up the sun's rays, wrapping me in its gentle warmth and reminding me of the beauty in the world. These fleeting moments, though they pass quickly, serve as sweet reminders of the abundance of goodness that surrounds me daily.

Entering these thoughts into my gratitude journal made me feel even more appreciative of the richness of my life and helped to improve my overall sense of well-being. It's amazing how taking a moment to acknowledge and express gratitude for the small joys can truly elevate our spirits and bring greater fulfillment into our lives.

INCORPORATING GRATITUDE INTO DAILY LIFE:

In addition to keeping a gratitude journal, there are many other ways to incorporate gratitude into your daily life. Simple acts like saying "thank you" to others, expressing appreciation for small gestures, or taking a moment to notice the beauty around you can all generate a sense of gratitude.

Living in the moment is a powerful way to practice gratitude. Pause throughout your day to fully experience the present moment, appreciating the sights, sounds, and sensations around you. Whether you're enjoying a leisurely walk in nature, savoring a delicious meal, or spending quality time with loved ones, immerse yourself fully in the experience. And remember, try to avoid getting lost in mindless scrolling or worrying about what's next—instead, focus on being present.

Notice the small details and take time to express gratitude for the simple pleasures that enrich your life. By cultivating mindfulness and being present in each moment, you can deepen your sense of gratitude and enhance your overall well-being.

Another way to weave gratitude into your everyday routine is through the practice of spontaneous acts of kindness. Set aside a moment to do something thoughtful for another person without seeking recognition or reward. Whether it's offering a genuine compliment to a colleague, assisting a neighbor with their chores, or surprising a stranger with a small gesture of kindness, these simple actions have the power to uplift someone else's spirits while amplifying a deep sense of gratitude within yourself.

PRACTICING GRATITUDE IN CHALLENGING TIMES:

Practicing gratitude during challenging times can be particularly impactful. While it may seem counterintuitive to feel thankful when facing adversity or loss, cultivating gratitude can provide a source of strength and resilience. In difficult moments, gratitude can help shift your focus from what's lacking to what's still present and valuable in your life.

During challenging times, focus on the lessons learned or the silver linings in the situation. Reflect on how the experience has helped you grow, what you've learned about yourself, or the unexpected positives that have emerged. By finding gratitude in the midst of adversity, you can foster a sense of resilience and hope.

Acknowledge and appreciate the support and kindness of others during difficult times. It's common to receive acts of kindness from friends, family, or even strangers when you're going through a tough time. Take a moment to express gratitude for these gestures, whether it's a listening ear, a helping hand, or a comforting presence. By recognizing and appreciating the support you receive, you can strengthen your relationships and feel less alone in your struggles.

EXPRESSING GRATITUDE IN RELATIONSHIPS:

Gratitude isn't just a solo practice—it's also a powerful tool for strengthening relationships and furthering connections. When you express gratitude toward others, you not only make them feel appreciated but also deepen your bond with them. Whether it's a partner, friend, family member, or colleague, expressing gratitude can strengthen your relationship and enhance mutual trust and understanding.

Make a habit of expressing appreciation regularly in your relationships. Take time each day to acknowledge something you appreciate about the people in your life. It could be a specific action they've taken, a quality you admire, or simply their presence in your life. By verbalizing your appreciation, you show that you value and cherish their contributions to your life. For example, you might say, "Thank you for your invaluable assistance at work today; your support made a meaningful difference, and I'm truly grateful."

Write heartfelt thank-you notes to express your gratitude to the people in your life. Whether it's a handwritten letter, an email, or a text message, taking the time to articulate your gratitude in writing can have a profound impact on both you and the recipient. Not only does it strengthen your connection with the other person, but it also reinforces your own sense of gratitude and appreciation.

PRACTICAL EXERCISES FOR DEVELOPING GRATITUDE:

Let's dive into some easy exercises to boost your gratitude game. These activities are all about noticing the good stuff in your life and saying 'thanks' in simple but powerful ways.

Three Good Things Exercise: Each day, take a few minutes to reflect on three things you're grateful for. Write them down in your gratitude journal or simply reflect on them in your mind. These could be simple things like a beautiful sunset, a delicious meal, or a kind gesture from a friend.

A Gratitude Letter: Take some time to write a heartfelt thank-you letter to someone who has had a positive impact on your life. Express your gratitude for their kindness, support, or friendship, and be specific about how their actions have made a difference to you. You can choose to deliver the letter in person or send it via mail or email.

A Gratitude Walk: Take a leisurely walk outdoors and pay attention to the sights, sounds, and sensations around you. Notice the beauty of nature, the warmth of the sun on your skin, or the sound of birds chirping. As you walk, take time to express gratitude for the simple pleasures of life and the beauty of the world around you.

A Gratitude Meditation: Set aside a few minutes each day to practice a gratitude meditation. Find a quiet and comfortable place to sit, close your eyes, and focus on your breath. As you breathe deeply, think of three things you're grateful for and visualize them in your mind. Allow yourself to experience feelings of gratitude and appreciation.

Gratitude Rituals: Create simple rituals or routines that remind you to cultivate gratitude throughout the day. For example, you can set a daily reminder on your phone to pause and reflect on something you're grateful for, or you can place a gratitude rock or object on your desk as a visual reminder to practice gratitude.

These exercises are not overly complex, but their impact is profound. Whether it's engaging in the *Three Good Things* Exercise, writing a heartfelt thank-you letter, enjoying a leisurely stroll in nature, or simply taking a moment to breathe and appreciate, each activity offers an opportunity to cultivate gratitude. Give them a try and observe how they enrich your perspective.

STORIES OF GRATITUDE IN ACTION:

In this section, we explore the impact of gratitude. Through the stories of two individuals, we see how saying thanks can make life better, bring people closer, and make everyday moments happier and more meaningful. Their stories remind us of the importance of saying thank you and appreciating the good things in life.

The Gratitude Jar:

Maya had always considered herself a positive person, but lately, she found herself feeling overwhelmed by the stresses of daily life. Between juggling work, family responsibilities, and personal challenges, she often felt like she was drowning in negativity. Determined to regain a sense of balance and perspective, Maya decided to start a gratitude jar.

Every evening, before going to bed, Maya would take a few moments to reflect on the day and write down three things she was grateful for on small slips of paper. Some days, it was as simple as a warm cup of tea on a chilly morning or a heartfelt conversation with a friend. Other days, it was more profound, like a breakthrough at work or a meaningful connection with her family.

As the weeks went by, Maya noticed a shift in her mindset. Instead of dwelling on what was going wrong in her life, she found herself focusing more on the pleasures and small moments of joy. The simple act of writing down her pleasures and placing them in the gratitude jar helped her cultivate a deeper sense of gratitude and appreciation for the good things in her life.

One day, during a particularly challenging week, Maya was feeling discouraged and overwhelmed. As she sat down to write in her gratitude journal, she found herself struggling to find anything positive to focus on. In a moment of frustration, she reached for the gratitude jar and began reading through the slips of paper.

As she read through the notes, Maya was reminded of all the good things in her life—the supportive friends, the loving family, the moments of joy and laughter. Tears filled her eyes as she realized how fortunate she truly was, despite the challenges she was facing. In that moment, she felt a profound sense of gratitude and peace wash over her, knowing that no matter what life threw her way, she had so much to be thankful for.

From that day forward, Maya recognized the importance of persisting in filling her gratitude jar with moments of joy, blessings, and gratitude. It remained a cherished practice that reminded her to focus on the good things in her life, even when times were tough. Through the simple act of cultivating gratitude, Maya found a sense of peace, joy, and fulfillment that transformed her outlook on life.

The Thank You Letter:

Mark had always been a busy man, constantly on the go with work, family, and personal commitments. In the hustle and bustle of daily life, he rarely took the time to pause and appreciate the people who made a difference in his life.

That all changed one day when he received a heartfelt thank-you letter from an old friend. The letter was unexpected, arriving out of the blue one morning. As Mark sat down at his desk to start his day, he opened the envelope and began to read.

He was surprised by the flood of memories the letter brought back—shared experiences, moments of laughter, and heartfelt conversations. He realized how much his friend's words meant to him and how much he valued their friendship.

In that moment, he felt a profound sense of gratitude for the people who had touched his life and made it richer and more meaningful.

Inspired by the thank-you letter, Mark decided to pay it forward by writing letters of gratitude to the people who had made a difference in his life. He wrote to his parents, expressing appreciation for their unwavering love and support. He wrote to his colleagues, acknowledging their hard work and dedication. He wrote to his children, expressing pride in their accomplishments and gratitude for the joy they brought into his life.

As he penned each letter, Mark felt a sense of gratitude and appreciation. He realized how fortunate he was to have so many wonderful people in his life and how important it was to express his gratitude for their presence. Through the simple act of writing thank-you letters, Mark deepened his connections with the people he cared about and cultivated a deeper sense of gratitude and appreciation for all the good in his life.

These two personal stories illustrate how cultivating gratitude can transform lives and deepen connections with others. Whether through the practice of keeping a gratitude jar or writing thank-you letters, the simple act of expressing gratitude can bring more joy, fulfillment, and meaning into our lives.

IN A NUTSHELL:

Cultivating gratitude is a powerful practice that not only boosts your own well-being but also brings positivity to those around you. By making gratitude a part of your daily routine, you'll notice significant improvements in your happiness, optimism, and overall satisfaction with life. So, make it a habit to pause each day, acknowledge the good things in your life, and express gratitude. These small changes will lead to a big impact, filling your heart with appreciation and spreading joy and abundance to both you and those you interact with.

CONTINUING EDUCATION RESOURCES FOR CULTIVATING GRATITUDE:

1. *Rise Above the Rut* by Jay Nesbit
2. *The Gratitude Diaries: How a Year Looking on the Bright Side Can Transform Your Life* by Janice Kaplan
3. *The Little Book of Gratitude: Create a Life of Happiness and Wellbeing by Giving Thanks* by Robert A. Emmons
4. *The Science of Happiness: How Gratitude, Kindness, and Hope Can Create a Fulfilling Life* by Sonja Lyubomirsky
5. *Gratitude: A Way of Life* by Louise L. Hay

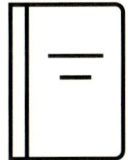

JOURNALING PROMPTS
FOR CULTIVATING GRATITUDE:

Journaling prompts are a great way to help you engage with the material and reflect on your own experiences. Here are two prompts for this chapter:

Journal Prompt 1: Reflect on three things you're grateful for in your life right now. They could be big or small, personal or universal. Take a moment to write down each one and explore why it's meaningful to you. How does acknowledging these sources of gratitude make you feel? Consider how you can incorporate more moments of gratitude into your daily routine to cultivate a greater sense of appreciation and fulfillment.

Journal Prompt 2: Think about a recent challenge or setback you've faced. How might approaching this situation with gratitude shift your perspective and empower you to find meaning or opportunity within the struggle? Take some time to write about the lessons you've learned from this experience and how expressing gratitude for the silver linings can help you grow stronger and more resilient in the face of adversity.

SMALL CHANGE 2:
PRACTICING KINDNESS

"No act of kindness, no matter how small, is ever wasted."

- AESOP

Kindness: Being friendly, generous, and thoughtful towards others.

***

In a world often overshadowed by negativity, practicing kindness lights up the path to a brighter, more compassionate existence. This chapter explores its significant impact on our well-being, relationships, and overall satisfaction with life.

Building upon the previous chapter's discussion on the potency of gratitude, we now explore another avenue for prompting happiness and flourishing—embracing acts of kindness. While gratitude and kindness share similarities in their ability to bring joy and fulfillment, they differ in their approach and impact.

While gratitude centers on appreciation for what we have, kindness focuses on extending generosity and compassion to others. Through this exploration, we'll uncover how both practices complement each other, amplifying their positive effects on our well-being and relationships.

WHY KINDNESS MATTERS:

Ever notice how kindness can brighten up even the darkest of days? In a world often marked by competition, stress, and division, kindness is like a ray of sunshine, offering hope, connection, and compassion. It's not just a polite gesture; it's woven into the fabric of who we are as humans and has this incredible power to change lives and communities for the better. And guess what? Science totally backs it up! (University of California, Berkeley, 2020; Cacioppo, J. T., Berntson, G. G., and Nusbaum, H. C, 2008)

Think about it: even the smallest acts of kindness, such as offering a helping hand or lending a listening ear, can profoundly brighten someone's day. And get this— research shows that being kind isn't just good for others; it's good for you, too! It can lower your stress levels, boost your mood, and make you feel more connected to others.

But it doesn't stop there. When we make kindness a priority in our interactions, we build stronger connections with those around us and create communities that are more resilient and supportive. It's like building a big, warm hug of a community where everyone feels valued and included. And let's be real—that's the kind of world we all want to live in, isn't it?

THE SCIENCE AND BENEFITS OF KINDNESS:

And yes, there is even more evidence from the science supporting the benefits of kindness. Researchers have been studying what happens in our brains and bodies when we're kind to others, and the results are pretty fascinating. (Nigel Mathers, 2016)

For starters, when you do something nice for someone else, your brain releases all these feel-good chemicals that make you feel happy and warm inside. It's like a little reward for being awesome! Plus, acts of kindness can have some serious long-term benefits, like reducing stress, improving your heart health, and making you more emotionally resilient. Who knew being kind could be so good for you, right?

And get this—when you're kind to others, it doesn't just make you feel good; it actually makes the whole neighborhood stronger, too. Studies have shown that areas with high levels of kindness and generosity have lower crime rates and better overall quality of life. So, by spreading kindness, you're not just making your own life better; you're making your community a better place for all.

CONNECTING WITH OTHERS THROUGH ACTS OF KINDNESS:

Let's talk about how we can connect with others through acts of kindness. Kindness isn't just about big gestures; it shows up in all sorts of ways, like helping out a friend, lending a hand at a local event, or simply being kind to us when things get rough. These acts aren't just good for others—they also strengthen our connections and fill us up with warmth and positivity.

When we spread kindness, we're not just brightening someone's day; we're deepening our bonds and advancing empathy and belonging. It's pretty clear that making kindness a habit can make life feel richer and bring us all closer together.

Understanding kindness means respecting others' experiences and treating everyone with kindness, regardless of our differences. Building a kinder world starts with small acts of compassion, like offering a kind word or a helping hand.

And don't forget about being kind to yourself too! Being gentle with ourselves, flaws and all, helps us bounce back from tough times and keep moving forward.

Incorporating kindness into our daily routines doesn't have to be complicated. It can be as simple as sharing a smile or giving ourselves a break when we mess up. By making kindness a part of our lives, we're making the world a little brighter, one small act at a time.

THE POWER OF KINDNESS IN RELATIONSHIPS:

The importance of kindness in relationships is huge! It's like the glue that holds our connections together and helps them thrive. Whether it's with our partner, friends, or family, acts of kindness build a strong foundation of trust, respect, and understanding that's super important for starting and keeping meaningful relationships going. From little gestures of care to big shows of love and gratitude, kindness keeps our relationships strong and makes them feel even closer and more fulfilling.

When we're consistently kind and understanding to our loved ones, we make our relationships a safe and loving place. It's where we can work through problems with care and respect and where everyone feels appreciated for who they are.

But kindness isn't just about one-on-one interactions. It also shapes the vibe of our whole social circle. When we make kindness a big deal in our relationships, it creates an atmosphere of trust, support, and empathy. That means everyone feels comfortable being themselves and sharing their feelings openly.

Basically, kindness in relationships helps us bond more deeply, build stronger trust, and create a loving space where everyone feels supported. When we make kindness a priority in how we treat each other and build a culture of caring and understanding, our relationships become super rewarding and meaningful for everyone involved.

TIPS FOR PRACTICING KINDNESS:

Here are a few practical tips that will help you build a culture of kindness that spreads positivity and leads to meaningful connections in your community and beyond:

Random Acts of Kindness: Engage in random acts of kindness by performing small, unexpected acts of kindness for others. Whether it's paying for someone's coffee, complimenting a stranger, or letting someone go ahead of you in line, these acts of kindness can brighten someone's day and create a ripple effect of positivity.

Volunteer in Your Community: Volunteer your time and talents to support causes and organizations that are meaningful to you. Whether it's volunteering at a local shelter, participating in a community clean-up event, or mentoring a young person, giving back to your community fosters a sense of connection and purpose.

Practice Active Listening: Practice active listening by giving others your full attention when they speak, without interrupting or judging. Show empathy and understanding by acknowledging their feelings and validating their experiences. This simple act of kindness can make a significant difference in someone's life.

Express Gratitude: In the previous chapter, we explored the power of gratitude in transforming our mindset and relationships. Take a moment to express gratitude toward others by acknowledging their kindness and contributions. Whether it's sending a thank-you note, giving a heartfelt compliment, or simply saying "I appreciate you," expressing gratitude promotes a culture of kindness and appreciation in our relationships.

Be Kind to Yourself: Practice self-kindness and self-compassion by treating yourself with the same care and understanding that you would offer to a friend in need. Practice self-care activities that nurture your physical, emotional, and mental well-being, such as meditation, exercise, and spending time in nature.

Incorporating kindness into your life doesn't have to be complicated. These useful tips not only brighten someone's day, including your own, but also expand a culture of kindness and appreciation in your relationships and community. So go ahead, spread a little kindness wherever you go, and watch as it comes back to you in unexpected and heartwarming ways.

PERSONAL STORIES OF PRACTICING KINDNESS:

Let's explore two inspiring anecdotes that highlight the meaningful power of practicing kindness in real-life situations:

The Power of a Simple Act:

John, a busy professional juggling the demands of work and family life, found himself feeling overwhelmed and disconnected from his community. One day, as he rushed through his morning routine, he noticed an elderly neighbor struggling to carry groceries up the stairs to her apartment. Without hesitation, John offered to help, carrying the bags upstairs and engaging in a brief conversation with his neighbor. As he witnessed the gratitude and relief in her eyes, John experienced a profound shift in perspective. He realized that even amidst his busy schedule, there were opportunities to make a meaningful difference in the lives of others.

In that simple act of kindness, John discovered a sense of purpose and connection that had been missing from his life. Inspired by the impact of his gesture, he began to seek out more ways to spread kindness in his community. Whether it was offering to mow a neighbor's lawn, donating his time to a local soup kitchen, or simply lending a listening ear to a friend in need, John found fulfillment in being of service to others. Each act of kindness not only brightened someone else's day but also brought joy and satisfaction to John himself.

John's story serves as a significant reminder of the ripple effect of kindness and the profound power of simple acts in creating a more compassionate and connected world.

The Ripple Effect of Compassion:

Samantha, a college student grappling with feelings of loneliness and isolation, found solace in volunteering at a local homeless shelter. Through her interactions with the shelter residents, Samantha discovered the life-changing power of compassion and connection. She listened to their stories, shared meals with them, and offered a listening ear and a compassionate heart. As Samantha immersed herself in the world of volunteering, she witnessed the ripple effect of kindness and compassion firsthand.

The acts of kindness she extended to others not only brought joy and comfort to the shelter residents but also enriched her own life in meaningful ways. Through practicing kindness, Samantha found a sense of purpose and fulfillment that transcended her own struggles and connected her to something greater than herself.

Inspired by the impact of her actions, Samantha began to notice the positive ripple effects spreading throughout the shelter community. From residents offering support to one another to fellow volunteers stepping up to lend a helping hand, Samantha saw how her initial acts of compassion had sparked a chain reaction of kindness and connection.

Samantha not only found a newfound sense of purpose and belonging but also became a catalyst for positive change within her community, demonstrating the enduring ripple effect of compassion and the power of one individual to make a difference.

IN A NUTSHELL:

It's evident that the tips we've discussed in this chapter are excellent examples of small changes that can make a big difference in improving your life and the lives of others. Practicing kindness isn't just a nice thing to do; it's a powerful tool for improving how we feel, connecting with others, and making the world a friendlier place. Whether it's helping someone out, being kind to one another, or being nice to others, every act of kindness can make a significant difference.

As we continue our journey toward personal growth and lasting happiness, let's wholeheartedly embrace the incredible power of kindness. Let's strive to make the world a better place, one small act of kindness at a time.

In our next chapter, we'll look at our third small change: staying positive. We'll explore how being optimistic can make us happier, stronger, and healthier. Using the latest research and advice, we'll show you simple ways to be more positive in your everyday life and how to deal with any challenges that come your way.

CONTINUING EDUCATION RESOURCES FOR PRACTICING KINDNESS:

1. *The How of Happiness: A New Approach to Getting the Life You Want* by Sonja Lyubomirsky
2. *The Compassionate Mind: A New Approach to Life's Challenges* by Paul Gilbert
3. *The Power of Kindness: The Unexpected Benefits of Leading a Compassionate Life* by Piero Ferrucci
4. *The Little Book of Kindness: Everyday actions to change your life and the world around you* by Bernadette Russell
5. *Random Acts of Kindness Then and Now: The 20th Anniversary of a Simple Idea That Changes Lives* by Editors of Conari Press

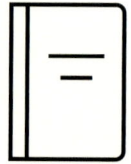

JOURNALING PROMPTS FOR PRACTICING KINDNESS:

Journaling prompts are a great way to help you engage with the material and reflect on your own experiences. Here are two prompts for this chapter:

Journal Prompt 1: Reflect on a recent act of kindness you've either given or received. How did it make you feel at that moment? Did it have any lasting impact on your mood, perspective, or relationship with the person involved? Consider how you can incorporate more intentional acts of kindness into your daily life, whether through small gestures or larger acts of generosity, and reflect on the potential ripple effects of spreading kindness in your community.

Journal Prompt 2: Imagine a world where kindness is the norm rather than the exception. What would it look like? How might a culture of kindness and compassion transform everyday interactions, relationships, and communities? Take some time to journal about your vision for this kinder world and brainstorm concrete steps you can take to contribute to its creation, starting with simple acts of kindness in your own sphere of influence.

SMALL CHANGE 3: NURTURING OPTIMISM

"Optimism is a happiness magnet. If you stay positive, good things and good people will be drawn to you."

- MARY LOU RETTON

Optimism: Having hope and confidence that things will turn out well.

***

Picture waking up to a world where each day feels like a chance to hit the reset button, where even the biggest hurdles hold secrets to unlock. In the last chapter, we discovered how acts of kindness can light up our lives and relationships. Now, get ready to hear about another game-changer: the power of optimism. It's like having a secret weapon in your back pocket, ready to turn even the gloomiest days into rays of sunshine.

THE MEANING AND BENEFITS OF OPTIMISM:

Optimism, often described as a positive mindset and a belief in favorable outcomes, is a fundamental aspect of how we perceive and interact with the world around us. This positive outlook not only shapes our responses to challenges but also influences our overall well-being and satisfaction with life.

Optimistic individuals tend to approach life's obstacles with a sense of hope and determination, viewing setbacks as temporary hurdles rather than insurmountable barriers. This mindset shift enables them to maintain a positive outlook and focus on finding solutions, ultimately leading to greater resilience and adaptability in the face of adversity.

In addition, optimistic individuals are more likely to engage in health-promoting behaviors such as regular exercise, balanced nutrition, and proactive healthcare, contributing to their overall happiness and longevity. By prioritizing their health and well-being, optimists create a foundation for a fulfilling and thriving life.

Moreover, optimism plays a vital role in fostering emotional resilience, allowing individuals to bounce back more quickly from disappointments and setbacks. Instead of dwelling on problems, optimistic individuals focus on identifying solutions and learning from their experiences. This adaptive coping mechanism not only helps them navigate life's ups and downs with greater ease but also enables them to maintain a positive outlook despite challenges.

RESEARCH ON THE BENEFITS OF OPTIMISM:

A wealth of research in psychology and related fields has demonstrated that optimism brings numerous benefits, supported by real-world evidence. One landmark study conducted by Seligman and his colleagues (2005) demonstrated that optimistic individuals are better equipped to cope with stress and adversity, leading to improved mental and physical health outcomes.

Furthermore, a longitudinal study published in the Journal of Personality and Social Psychology found that individuals with a positive outlook on life had a significantly lower risk of developing cardiovascular disease over a 15-year follow-up period (Kubzansky et al., 2001). This study highlights the long-term impact of optimism on physical health and underscores the importance of cultivating a positive mindset for overall well-being.

Moreover, research conducted by Carver, Scheier, and Segerstrom (2010) has shown that optimism is associated with greater persistence and achievement in goal pursuit. Optimistic individuals are more likely to set challenging goals, exert effort toward their attainment, and persevere in the face of obstacles, ultimately leading to greater success and fulfillment in life.

In essence, research and studies on optimism consistently demonstrate its profound impact on various aspects of life, from physical health and resilience to goal achievement and overall life satisfaction. By nurturing optimism, individuals can unlock the potential for a happier, healthier, and more fulfilling life.

STRATEGIES FOR DEVELOPING OPTIMISM:

While some individuals may naturally have a more optimistic disposition, optimism is a mindset that can be developed and grown through intentional practices and strategies.

I want to point out that as we go through these strategies for making small changes, you might notice that many of them share common elements. This is intentional. By mastering a handful of key skills, you'll find that you can apply them across various aspects of your life, making it simpler and more manageable to implement these small changes effectively across many of the fifteen small steps we'll discuss.

Here are some actionable steps for nurturing optimism in your daily life:

Practice Gratitude: As we explored in an earlier chapter, cultivating gratitude is a powerful way to shift your focus toward the positive aspects of life. Take time each day to reflect on the things you're grateful for, whether it's the support of loved ones, moments of joy and laughter, or the beauty of nature.

Challenge Negative Thoughts: Optimism involves challenging and reframing negative thoughts and beliefs that may contribute to pessimism. When faced with a negative situation or setback, ask yourself if there are alternative explanations or potential silver linings. By reframing negative thoughts in a more positive light, you can cultivate a more optimistic outlook.

Set Realistic Goals: Setting and pursuing realistic goals that align with your values and aspirations can foster a sense of purpose and optimism. Break larger goals down into smaller, manageable steps, and celebrate your progress along the way. By focusing on achievable objectives, you can build momentum and confidence in your ability to create positive change in your life.

Surround Yourself with Positivity: Surround yourself with supportive and optimistic individuals who uplift and inspire you. Seek out communities and social networks that promote positivity and encouragement, whether it's through in-person interactions or online forums and groups. By surrounding yourself with positivity, you can reinforce and strengthen your own optimistic mindset.

Optimism isn't reserved for just a lucky few—it's something you can build for yourself! By being thankful, changing negative thoughts, setting achievable goals, and being around positive folks, you can train your brain to see the good stuff even when life gets tough. It's not about ignoring problems but about facing them with hope and believing things will get better. So, whether you're a natural optimist or not, trying out these tips can make you feel happier and more hopeful for the future.

Using Optimism in Everyday Life:

Now that we've discussed the benefits of nurturing optimism and explored various strategies for advancing a more positive mindset, let's take a closer look at how optimism can be applied in practical ways to enhance our daily lives.

Optimism in Relationships: Being optimistic can really change how we get along with others. Next time you have a disagreement with a friend or loved one, try to approach it with understanding instead of defensiveness. Listen to their side of the story and focus on finding a solution together rather than dwelling on past issues. Optimistic people focus on fixing problems rather than holding onto grudges, which helps us communicate better and build stronger connections.

Optimism in the Workplace: Being optimistic isn't just good for our personal lives—it's also super helpful in the workplace. If you encounter a setback at your job, instead of getting discouraged, take a moment to think about what you can learn from the situation and how you can bounce back. Maybe even brainstorm with your colleagues to come up with creative solutions. People with an optimistic mindset bounce back quickly from tough situations and keep working hard. Plus, when everyone's feeling positive, it makes for a great work atmosphere where people support each other and come up with fresh ideas.

Optimism in Health and Wellness: Staying positive isn't just good for our mood—it's also good for our health. Start by setting a small health goal for yourself, like going for a walk a few times a week or adding an extra serving of veggies to your meals. Then, focus on the positive changes you notice in how you feel, which can motivate you to keep up the good habits. Research shows that optimistic people are more likely to do things that keep them healthy, like exercising and eating well. By taking care of themselves, optimists can stay healthier and live better lives.

Optimism in Personal Growth: Being optimistic can really help us grow as people. Think about a goal you've been wanting to achieve but have been hesitant to pursue. Break it down into smaller, more manageable steps and take one small action toward it each day. Remind yourself of your progress and stay positive even when things get tough. Optimistic folks set big goals and keep going even when things get tough. By staying positive and believing in themselves, they can reach their full potential and feel more fulfilled.

Optimism in Adversity: When life gets hard, optimistic people are really good at staying positive and finding the good in tough situations. The next time you face a challenging situation, try to look for one positive aspect or lesson you can take away from it, no matter how small. By focusing on the silver lining, you can maintain a sense of hope and resilience even in difficult times. It helps them stay strong and come out even better on the other side.

By using optimism in these ways, we can make our lives happier, healthier, and more satisfying. Embracing positivity and staying hopeful helps us deal with challenges, build strong relationships, and reach our goals with confidence.

OVERCOMING PESSIMISM:

Despite the plethora of perks that come with optimism, let's face it: we all know a few folks who seem to have a black cloud following them around. Yep, we're talking about those die-hard pessimists. You know the type—always seeing the glass as half empty and expecting a rainstorm on their parade.

Heck, maybe you've even caught yourself slipping into that pessimistic mindset once or twice. But fear not! Even though pessimism might try to throw a wrench in our plans, with a little elbow grease and some savvy coping strategies, we can kick those gloomy clouds to the curb.

One effective approach for overcoming pessimism is cognitive restructuring, a technique that involves identifying and challenging negative thought patterns and then replacing them with more adaptive and optimistic beliefs. Reframing and challenging your thoughts are integral parts of cognitive restructuring. Reframing means looking at a situation from a different angle to see the positive side of things, while challenging your thoughts involves questioning negative beliefs and replacing them with more realistic and upbeat ones.

By practicing cognitive restructuring techniques such as cognitive reframing and thought challenging, individuals can learn to recognize and challenge pessimistic thoughts, ultimately replacing them with more positive and realistic perspectives (J. Elmer, Healthline.com, 2023).

Cognitive restructuring isn't as complex as it sounds—it's basically like hitting the refresh button on your brain. You take those gloomy, defeatist thoughts and give them a good shake, swapping them out for brighter, more hopeful ones. It's all about training your mind to see the silver linings instead of getting stuck in the storm clouds.

Additionally, creating a state of mindfulness through practices such as meditation and mindfulness-based stress reduction can help individuals become more aware of their thoughts and emotions and develop greater emotional regulation skills. Mindfulness encourages individuals to observe their thoughts and feelings without judgment and develop a more compassionate and accepting attitude toward themselves and others, which can counteract pessimistic tendencies.

Furthermore, seeking support from mental health professionals such as therapists or counselors can provide individuals with the tools and strategies they need to overcome pessimism and encourage a more optimistic outlook on life. *Cognitive behavioral therapy* (CBT) and positive psychology interventions are evidence-based approaches that can help individuals challenge negative thought patterns, develop coping skills, and improve their optimism and resilience.

Incorporating these strategies into your daily life can help you overcome pessimism and bring on a more optimistic mindset that increases happiness, resilience, and fulfillment. By challenging negative thought patterns, setting realistic goals, surrounding yourself with positivity, and seeking support when needed, you can stimulate optimism and embrace the possibilities for a brighter and more fulfilling future.

PERSONAL STORIES OF NURTURING OPTIMISM:

Let's look at two uplifting personal stories that show how optimism can make a big difference in real life.

The Power of Perspective Shift:

Lina, a young professional facing the challenges of finding a job in a competitive market, felt disheartened by constant rejections and setbacks. Despite her qualifications and efforts, securing meaningful employment seemed out of reach, leading her to doubt herself.

However, a chance meeting with a mentor changed everything. The mentor encouraged Lina to shift her perspective and focus on her strengths and achievements. Inspired by this advice, Lina began to see each rejection as an opportunity for growth rather than a setback. She started to view her job search with renewed optimism, determined to turn obstacles into stepping stones.

Lina took proactive steps to improve her situation. She expanded her professional network by attending networking events and reaching out to contacts for advice and opportunities. Additionally, she enrolled in skill development courses to enhance her expertise and make herself more marketable to employers. With each rejection, Lina remained resilient, using feedback to refine her approach and showcase her value.

Through her perseverance and optimism, Lina eventually landed a job that aligned with her passions and aspirations. This success not only brought her professional fulfillment but also strengthened her belief in the power of optimism and resilience in overcoming challenges.

Finding Hope in Adversity:

Ethan, a cancer survivor facing the challenges of his illness, found hope and strength in staying positive during his recovery journey. With treatments that left him feeling drained and uncertain about what the future held, Ethan knew he needed to keep his spirits up.

Throughout his treatment, Ethan made a conscious effort to find joy in the little things each day. Whether it was enjoying a sunny day, sharing a laugh with loved ones, or simply savoring a good meal, Ethan found solace in these moments of happiness amidst the chaos of his illness.

But it wasn't just about finding joy; Ethan also surrounded himself with a strong support system. His friends and family rallied around him, offering words of encouragement, lending a helping hand, and providing the emotional support he needed to stay optimistic. Their unwavering presence reminded Ethan that he was not alone in his battle and gave him the strength to keep fighting.

Despite the ups and downs of his journey, Ethan remained steadfast in his belief that better days were ahead. He embraced each setback as an opportunity for growth and reflection, learning valuable lessons about resilience, gratitude, and the importance of cherishing every moment.

Through his unwavering optimism and resilience, Ethan not only survived his battle with cancer but emerged from it with a newfound appreciation for life. His journey serves as a powerful reminder of the transformative power of hope and positivity in overcoming life's greatest challenges.

IN A NUTSHELL:

Nurturing optimism isn't just about seeing the glass half full—it's about finding strength and hope in every challenge life throws our way. By embracing practices like mindfulness, gratitude, and overcoming common obstacles, we can cultivate a positive mindset that empowers us to thrive despite the ups and downs.

Whether it's finding joy in the little things, surrounding ourselves with supportive people, or seeking help when we need it, optimism is a secret weapon that can help us weather any storm and emerge stronger on the other side. So, let's keep our heads up, our hearts open, and our spirits high as we journey through life with hope and resilience.

As we embrace the power of optimism, it naturally leads us to consider the importance of forgiveness as another pathway to greater inner peace, healing, and emotional well-being. In the next chapter, we'll explore practical strategies for practicing forgiveness and letting go of resentment and anger on our journey toward lasting happiness and overall well-being. Join us as we continue to navigate life's challenges with a mindset of hope, resilience, and compassion.

CONTINUING EDUCATION RESOURCES FOR NURTURING OPTIMISM:

1. *Learned Optimism: How to Change Your Mind and Your Life* by Martin E. P. Seligman
2. *The Optimistic Child: A Proven Program to Safeguard Children Against Depression and Build Lifelong Resilience* by Martin E. P. Seligman

3. *The Resilience Factor: 7 Keys to Finding Your Inner Strength and Overcoming Life's Hurdles* by Karen Reivich and Andrew Shatte

4. *The Power of Positive Thinking* by Norman Vincent Peale

5. *The Happiness Advantage: How a Positive Brain Fuels Success in Work and Life* by Shawn Achor

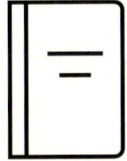

JOURNALING PROMPTS FOR NURTURING OPTIMISM:

Journaling prompts are a great way to help you engage with the material and reflect on your own experiences. Here are two prompts for this chapter:

Journal Prompt 1: Reflect on a recent challenge or setback you've encountered. How did you initially respond to the situation—was your mindset more optimistic or pessimistic? Consider how your perspective influenced your emotional response and subsequent actions. What lessons can you learn from this experience about the power of optimism in navigating life's obstacles? How might adopting a more optimistic outlook have changed your approach to handling the situation?

Journal Prompt 2: Imagine waking up each morning with a renewed sense of optimism and possibility, eager to embrace whatever the day may bring. What changes could this shift in mindset bring to your daily life? Take some time to journal about the potential benefits of cultivating optimism, both for your personal well-being and your interactions with others. Then, brainstorm concrete steps you can take to foster a more optimistic outlook, such as practicing gratitude, reframing negative thoughts, or seeking out sources of inspiration and positivity in your environment.

SMALL CHANGE 4:
LEARNING TO FORGIVE

"To forgive is to set a prisoner free and discover that the prisoner was you."

- LEWIS B. SMEDES

Forgiveness: Letting go of anger toward someone who hurt you and replacing it with positive thoughts and feelings.

***

Forgiveness unfolds like a gentle breeze, lifting the weight of grudges, allowing one to breathe freely, and nurturing the garden of life to bloom with newfound beauty. In the previous chapter, we uncovered the myriad benefits associated with nurturing optimism, from improved physical health and resilience to greater overall life satisfaction. Now, our focus shifts to another essential aspect of acquiring a fulfilling life—learning to forgive.

FORGIVENESS FOR PERSONAL GROWTH AND DEVELOPMENT:

Forgiveness serves as a catalyst for personal growth and development by freeing us from the shackles of resentment and anger. When we let go of past hurts and grievances, we create space for new opportunities and experiences. By embracing forgiveness as a tool for personal growth, we can develop resilience, compassion, and empathy, leading to a more fulfilling and meaningful life.

For example, imagine a scenario where someone holds onto resentment toward a coworker for past disagreements. This resentment creates tension in the workplace, affecting productivity and morale. However, by choosing to forgive and let go of the grudge, they open themselves up to better communication and collaboration with their coworker.

This shift in mindset not only improves their working relationship but also allows them to focus on their personal and professional growth without being weighed down by negative emotions.

THE RELATIONSHIP BETWEEN FORGIVENESS AND SELF-COMPASSION:

Practicing forgiveness encourages self-compassion and self-love by allowing us to release feelings of guilt and self-blame. When we forgive ourselves for past mistakes and shortcomings, we bring about greater self-acceptance and inner peace.

By embracing forgiveness as a pathway to self-compassion, we can learn to treat ourselves with kindness and understanding, facilitating a deeper sense of emotional well-being and fulfillment. This practice of self-forgiveness opens the door to greater self-awareness and personal growth, empowering individuals to move forward with grace and resilience.

For instance, consider a person who blames themself for a failed relationship. They may harbor guilt and self-blame, hindering their ability to progress and find happiness. However, by practicing self-forgiveness, they acknowledge their imperfections and embrace self-compassion. This shift in mindset allows them to learn from the experience, grow personally, and approach future relationships with greater understanding and resilience.

THE IMPACT OF FORGIVENESS ON WELL-BEING:

Over the years, numerous scientific studies have explored the impact of learning to forgive on our overall well-being. These studies have shed light on its profound psychological and physiological benefits. These studies provide compelling evidence supporting the breakthrough power of forgiveness in promoting emotional healing and resilience.

One notable study conducted by Fred Luskin and colleagues (2001) at Stanford University examined the effects of forgiveness interventions on psychological well-being. Participants who engaged in forgiveness practices reported reductions in feelings of anger, anxiety, and depression, along with improvements in overall life satisfaction. These findings highlight the therapeutic benefits of forgiveness for enhancing mental health outcomes.

Furthermore, research by Everett Worthington and colleagues (2007) demonstrated the physiological effects of forgiveness on cardiovascular health. In their study, participants who underwent forgiveness training showed significant reductions in blood pressure and heart rate variability, indicating a lower risk of cardiovascular disease.

These findings suggest that forgiveness not only benefits our emotional well-being but also has tangible effects on physical health.

Moreover, studies have shown that forgiveness interventions can lead to improvements in interpersonal relationships and social connectedness. A study by Julie Exline and colleagues (2014) found that forgiveness interventions enhanced feelings of empathy and compassion toward others, fostering greater intimacy and trust in relationships. This research underscores the role of forgiveness in building resilient and meaningful connections with others, also contributing to overall well-being.

Additionally, longitudinal studies have provided evidence of the long-term benefits of forgiveness for psychological adjustment and life satisfaction. A study by Loren Toussaint and colleagues (2016) followed participants over a ten-year period and found that those who were able to forgive reported greater psychological well-being and lower levels of stress over time. These findings highlight forgiveness as a protective factor against the negative effects of stress and adversity, promoting resilience and emotional well-being.

Overall, the scientific evidence overwhelmingly supports the benefits of learning to forgive for our overall well-being. From improvements in mental health outcomes to tangible effects on physical health and interpersonal relationships, forgiveness plays a crucial role in promoting emotional healing, resilience, and life satisfaction. By embracing forgiveness as a regular practice, we can harness its positive influence to pursue greater well-being and fulfillment in our lives.

OVERCOMING COMMON OBSTACLES TO FORGIVENESS:

Despite the profound benefits of forgiveness, many individuals struggle with common obstacles such as fear, pride, and a desire for justice or revenge. By identifying and addressing these obstacles, we can expand our courage and willingness to forgive ourselves and others. Through mindfulness practices, self-reflection, and compassionate understanding, we can overcome the barriers to forgiveness and experience the profound liberation it offers.

Consider a person who has been deeply hurt by a friend's betrayal. Initially, they may feel overwhelmed by anger and resentment, making forgiveness seem impossible. However, through self-reflection, they begin to understand the root causes of their friend's actions and empathize with their struggles.

Armed with this compassionate understanding, they gradually let go of their desire for revenge and choose to forgive. As they release their resentment, they experience a sense of peace and freedom, paving the way for healing and reconciliation in their relationship.

STRATEGIES TO PRACTICE FORGIVENESS IN DAILY LIFE:

Forgiveness can be tough, but there are ways to make it easier. Let's break it down into some simple steps you can take every day:

Practice Empathy: Empathy means understanding how someone else feels. Imagine yourself in their shoes. Maybe they didn't mean to hurt you, or they were going through a tough time themselves.

Develop Self-Compassion: Self-compassion is about being kind to yourself. Treat yourself gently, like you would a friend who made a mistake. Recognize that we all mess up sometimes.

Engage in Mindfulness: Mindfulness means being aware of your thoughts and feelings without judging them. Take a moment to breathe and be present. This can help you stay calm and open-minded, making forgiveness feel more natural.

Practice Gratitude: Gratitude is about focusing on the good things in your life, even when it's hard. By counting your blessings, you can shift your perspective and let go of negativity.

Seek Support: Don't try to handle everything on your own. Talk to friends, family, or a therapist if you need help. Sharing your feelings can lighten the load and make forgiveness seem less daunting.

By incorporating these practical strategies into our daily lives, we can produce a mindset of forgiveness and harness its significant benefits for our overall well-being.

FORGIVENESS IN BUILDING STRONG RELATIONSHIPS:

Let's talk about the power of forgiveness in making our relationships rock solid! Picture this: your friend accidentally says something that stings a bit. Instead of stewing in hurt feelings and pulling away, forgiving them opens up a chance to talk it out.

By speaking up about how you feel and forgiving their slip-up, you're not just patching things up. You're actually strengthening your bond and making room for both of you to grow.

Forgiveness isn't just about saying sorry and moving on. It's about ditching the grudges that can poison our connections. When we're quick to forgive, we create an atmosphere of support and understanding where real, heartfelt relationships can blossom.

So, next time a little bump comes along in your friendships, remember that forgiveness isn't just a Band-Aid—it's the glue that keeps those bonds strong and thriving!

CULTURAL AND SPIRITUAL PERSPECTIVES ON FORGIVENESS:

Forgiveness holds diverse cultural and spiritual significance, reflecting its universal importance in promoting healing and reconciliation. For instance, in many Indigenous cultures, forgiveness is integral to restoring balance and harmony within communities through practices like circle sentencing and healing circles. These restorative justice methods emphasize forgiveness as a means to address harm and bring about healing on a communal level.

Moreover, forgiveness holds a central place in various spiritual traditions, offering a transformative pathway to compassion and grace. For instance, in Buddhism, forgiveness is viewed as a practice of letting go of anger and resentment, leading to inner peace and spiritual growth. Similarly, in Islam, forgiveness is encouraged as a means of attaining mercy and closeness to God, as exemplified by the concept of "pardoning and overlooking" offenses.

By exploring these diverse perspectives, we gain a deeper understanding of forgiveness as a universal concept that transcends cultural and religious boundaries. Whether through Indigenous practices, Buddhist teachings, or Islamic principles, forgiveness emerges as a powerful force for healing and reconciliation, offering individuals and communities a path toward peace and wholeness.

PERSONAL STORIES OF FORGIVENESS:

Let's explore two inspiring anecdotes that illustrate the healing and redemptive power of forgiveness in real-life situations:

The Healing Power of Forgiveness:

Meet Emily, a remarkable survivor of childhood trauma and abuse. For years, Emily carried the heavy burden of anger and resentment toward her abuser. The pain from her past experiences weighed heavily on her, casting a shadow over her relationships and overall well-being.

But Emily's story takes a turn when she decides to confront her pain head-on. With the support of therapy and through deep self-reflection, Emily embarks on a courageous journey of forgiveness and healing.

At first, forgiveness seemed like an impossible feat. How could she forgive someone who had caused her so much pain? Yet, as Emily probed deeper into her own emotions and experiences, she began to realize that holding onto anger and resentment only kept her chained to the past.

Slowly but steadily, Emily started to let go. She released the grip of bitterness that had consumed her for so long. In its place, she discovered a profound sense of liberation and inner peace.

Forgiveness became Emily's beacon of light in the darkness. It was her key to breaking free from the cycle of victimhood and reclaiming her power and agency. By forgiving her abuser, Emily took back control of her own narrative.

But forgiveness wasn't just about letting go of the past. It was also about embracing the present and forging a path toward a brighter future. Through forgiveness, Emily not only healed her past wounds but also discovered a newfound sense of empowerment and resilience.

Her journey wasn't easy, and there were moments of doubt and fear along the way. Yet, with each step forward, Emily grew stronger. She realized that forgiveness wasn't a sign of weakness but rather a testament to her strength and courage.

Today, Emily's story serves as a powerful reminder of the life-changing impact of forgiveness. It's a reminder that no matter how deep the wounds or how long the pain has lingered, healing is possible. And it all begins with the simple but profound act of forgiveness.

Reconciliation and Redemption:

Meet Mateo, a devoted father of two who battled addiction for many years, leaving a trail of strain and turmoil within his family. His struggles led to deep wounds and feelings of betrayal among his loved ones, resulting in years of estrangement and resentment.

But Mateo refused to let his past define him. With a newfound commitment to sobriety and a burning desire to mend his broken relationships, he embarked on a courageous journey of reconciliation and redemption.

Mateo knew that simply saying sorry wouldn't be enough. He needed to demonstrate genuine remorse and a willingness to make amends. So, armed with humility and determination, Mateo began by opening up to his family, sharing the raw truth about his struggles and the pain he had caused.

His honesty was met with a mix of skepticism and cautious hope from his family. They had been hurt before, and forgiveness didn't come easily. But Mateo persisted, showing through his actions that he was truly dedicated to change.

Slowly but surely, trust began to rebuild. Through countless heartfelt conversations and moments of vulnerability, Mateo and his family started to bridge the chasm that had separated them for so long.

Forgiveness didn't come overnight, but with each step forward, the wounds of the past began to heal. Mateo's family recognized the sincerity of his efforts and chose to extend forgiveness, not because it was easy, but because they saw the genuine transformation taking place within him.

As forgiveness took root, Mateo and his family experienced a profound sense of healing and reconciliation. The walls that had once divided them crumbled away, replaced by a newfound closeness and understanding.

Today, Mateo's story stands as a testament to the power of reconciliation and redemption. It's a reminder that no matter how far we may have strayed or how deep our wounds may be, it's never too late to seek forgiveness and rebuild what was broken. And through forgiveness, we can pave the way for a brighter and more hopeful future together.

IN A NUTSHELL:

Forgiving isn't always easy, but it's like cleaning out your emotional closet, making space for peace and happiness to shine. It's about being kind and strong, not just for yourself, but for everyone around you.

In this chapter, we've explored how forgiveness can set us free from anger and help us feel enhanced. We've seen how it's not just about saying sorry but about making things better. So, let's keep going and see how we can make our lives even happier!

Next up, we'll discuss why investing in relationships is crucial. It's like planting seeds for a garden of happiness. Get ready to learn how connections can make your life more fun and meaningful!

CONTINUING EDUCATION RESOURCES FOR LEARNING TO FORGIVE:

1. *The Book of Forgiving: The Fourfold Path for Healing Ourselves and Our World* by Desmond Tutu and Mpho Tutu
2. *Forgive for Good: A Proven Prescription for Health and Happiness* by Fred Luskin
3. *The Power of Forgiveness: Forgiving as a Path to Freedom* by Joan Gattuso
4. *Forgiveness: How to Make Peace With Your Past and Get on With Your Life* by Sidney B. Simon and Suzanne Simon
5. *The Art of Forgiveness, Lovingkindness, and Peace* by Jack Kornfield

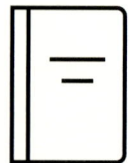

JOURNALING PROMPTS FOR LEARNING TO FORGIVE:

Journaling prompts are a great way to help you engage with the material and reflect on your own experiences. Here are two prompts for this chapter:

Journal Prompt 1: Reflect on an experience where you felt hurt or wronged by someone close to you. How did holding onto feelings of anger or resentment affect your emotional well-being and relationships? Take some time to explore the possibility of forgiveness as a pathway to healing and personal growth. What barriers or obstacles might be preventing you from letting go of these negative emotions? How can you begin to cultivate a mindset of forgiveness and release the burden of grudges in order to create space for positive growth and new opportunities in your life?

Journal Prompt 2: Imagine yourself one year from now, having fully embraced the practice of forgiveness in your daily life. How does it feel to let go of past hurts and grievances and replace them with feelings of compassion and understanding? Take a moment to visualize the impact of forgiveness on your relationships, your sense of inner peace, and your overall well-being. Then, write down three actionable steps you can take today to start the journey toward forgiveness and personal growth, whether it's through self-reflection, communication with others, or seeking support from a trusted friend or counselor.

SMALL CHANGE 5:
INVESTING IN RELATIONSHIPS

"Make new friends, but keep the old; Those are silver, these are gold."

- JOSEPH PARRY

Relationship: An emotional connection between two people, which can be good or bad.

***

Relationships are like the threads that weave together the fabric of our lives, connecting us to others in ways both ordinary and extraordinary. As we progress on the path to living our best life, we shift from exploring the forward-looking act of forgiveness to examining the fundamental aspect of a joyful life: investing in relationships and strengthening our connections with others.

Relationships, defined as the connections and bonds we form with family, friends, colleagues, and romantic partners, play a crucial role in shaping our experiences and well-being. They're like the glue that holds our lives together, making the good times better and helping us through the tough stuff, too.

BUILDING AND MAINTAINING MEANINGFUL CONNECTIONS:

Building and maintaining meaningful connections with others is essential for our well-being and overall happiness. Meaningful relationships provide us with a sense of belonging, support, and companionship, enriching our lives in countless ways. Whether it's with family members, friends, or romantic partners, investing time and effort into strengthening these connections is crucial for our emotional and mental health.

For example, consider the friendship between two close friends. Despite living in different cities, they make a conscious effort to stay connected through regular phone calls, video chats, and visits. They prioritize their friendship by scheduling quality time together, sharing their joys and challenges, and supporting each other through life's ups and downs. By investing in their relationship and maintaining meaningful connections, these friends have created a supportive and fulfilling friendship that brings joy and companionship to their lives.

RESEARCH ON THE VALUE OF RELATIONSHIPS:

Research consistently demonstrates the significant impact of relationships on our overall well-being and quality of life. Studies have shown that maintaining healthy relationships contributes to greater happiness, reduced stress levels, and improved physical health (Holt-Lunstad et al., 2010).

Also, a longitudinal study published in the Journal of Health and Social Behavior found that individuals with strong social connections have a lower risk of mortality compared to those who are socially isolated (House, Landis, & Umberson, 1988). The support and companionship provided by meaningful relationships play a crucial role in buffering against the negative effects of stress and promoting resilience in the face of adversity.

Additionally, research in the field of positive psychology highlights the importance of relationships in enriching personal growth and fulfillment. Positive relationships serve as a source of emotional support, encouragement, and validation, enabling individuals to pursue their goals and aspirations with confidence (Lyubomirsky et al., 2005). A study published in the Journal of Happiness Studies found that individuals with supportive and fulfilling relationships report higher levels of life satisfaction and overall well-being (Dush & Amato, 2005).

Plus, the quality of our relationships significantly influences our psychological and emotional health. Research has shown that positive social interactions and meaningful connections with others contribute to greater feelings of happiness, belonging, and purpose in life (Diener & Seligman, 2002). Conversely, lack of social support and interpersonal conflict can have detrimental effects on mental health and contribute to feelings of loneliness and isolation (Cacioppo & Patrick, 2008).

In summary, hanging out with friends not only makes us feel good but also keeps our stress levels in check and might even help us live longer! Plus, having people who've got our backs can seriously boost our happiness and sense of purpose.

On the flip side, feeling lonely or having lots of drama in our relationships can really take a toll on our mental health. So, bottom line? Prioritizing those meaningful connections is key to living our best lives and staying strong through whatever life throws our way.

EFFECTIVE COMMUNICATION IN RELATIONSHIPS:

Effective communication is the cornerstone of healthy and fulfilling relationships. By practicing active listening, empathy, and vulnerability, we can foster deeper connections with others and strengthen our bonds. Effective communication involves not only expressing our thoughts and feelings honestly and openly but also listening attentively and empathetically to the perspectives and feelings of others. By prioritizing open and honest communication in our relationships, we can create an environment of trust, respect, and understanding.

For instance, consider the relationship between two colleagues at work. When one of them was going through a difficult time, he reached out to the other for support. Instead of offering unsolicited advice or trying to fix the problem, the colleague listened empathetically to his concerns and offered a listening ear. By practicing active listening and empathy, the colleague strengthened his bond with the other and deepened their professional relationship. Effective communication allowed the individual to feel heard and supported, building trust and collaboration in their work dynamic.

Effective communication in relationships is not just about speaking; it's about truly connecting with others on a deeper level. It involves being present, listening with empathy, and being willing to be vulnerable. When we communicate effectively, we create a safe space for honest expression and understanding. This process not only helps us resolve conflicts but also strengthens our connections and enables mutual respect. By being open and receptive to each other's perspectives, we can build stronger, more fulfilling relationships built on trust and empathy.

THE SIGNIFICANCE OF QUALITY TIME IN RELATIONSHIPS:

Spending meaningful time together is crucial for building and maintaining strong relationships. Quality time offers a chance for individuals to connect deeply, communicate openly, and forge lasting memories.

Here are some key aspects highlighting why quality time matters in relationships:

Building Connection: Sharing meaningful experiences, engaging in activities together, and enjoying each other's company helps build intimacy and strengthens the emotional bond between individuals.

Enhancing Communication: Quality time provides an opportunity for honest and open conversations, allowing individuals to exchange thoughts, feelings, and experiences, thereby deepening their understanding of each other.

Creating Memories: Shared experiences during quality time form lasting memories that individuals can treasure and reminisce about. Whether it's exploring new places or celebrating milestones together, these shared moments contribute to the relationship's foundation.

Furthering Appreciation: Investing time and attention in each other during quality moments allows individuals to express gratitude and reinforce the value they place on the relationship, demonstrating commitment and mutual respect.

By making quality time a priority in their relationships, individuals can nurture connection, improve communication, and deepen appreciation, ultimately enhancing the health and longevity of their relationships.

THE ROLE OF BOUNDARIES IN RELATIONSHIPS:

Establishing and maintaining healthy boundaries is crucial for maintaining positive and fulfilling relationships. Boundaries define the limits of acceptable behavior and help ensure mutual respect, safety, and emotional well-being within relationships. Without clear boundaries, relationships can become strained, leading to conflicts and misunderstandings.

Here are some key points to consider regarding boundaries in relationships:

Defining Personal Boundaries: Each individual has unique needs, preferences, and comfort levels when it comes to interpersonal interactions. Defining personal boundaries involves identifying what feels comfortable and acceptable in various situations and communicating these boundaries to others.

Respecting Boundaries: Once boundaries are established, it's essential for both parties to respect and honor each other's boundaries. This involves listening to and acknowledging each other's needs and preferences, even if they differ from our own.

Setting Boundaries in Different Relationships: Boundaries may vary depending on the nature of the relationship. For example, boundaries in a romantic relationship may differ from those in a professional or familial relationship. It's important to adapt boundaries accordingly to ensure healthy dynamics in each type of relationship.

Communicating Boundaries: Open and honest communication is key to setting and maintaining boundaries in relationships. Clearly expressing boundaries allows both parties to understand each other's expectations and ensures that each person feels respected and valued.

By setting clear boundaries and respecting them in relationships, individuals create a safe and supportive space where both parties feel understood and valued, boosting the emotional well-being of everyone involved.

HANDLING CONFLICT IN RELATIONSHIPS:

Conflict is inevitable in any relationship. It is like that unwelcome guest who shows up uninvited to every relationship party, but here's the thing: how we deal with it can either make or break the bond we share.

Picture this: you and your sibling are at odds over holiday plans. Instead of diving headfirst into a shouting match, you both hit the brakes and decide to approach the situation with a hefty dose of empathy.

You take turns listening, really listening, to each other's concerns and feelings. And guess what? By putting yourselves in each other's shoes, you're able to find a solution that works for both of you.

See, it's all about understanding where the other person is coming from and finding common ground, even when it feels like you're on opposite sides of the fence. This way, you not only keep the peace but also strengthen your relationship in the process.

BUILDING TRUST AND INTIMACY:

Trust and intimacy are like the secret sauce that makes relationships truly special. It's all about being reliable, honest, and totally open with each other. By consistently showing up and being real, we build trust that forms the backbone of our connections with others.

Now, imagine a married couple facing some serious hurdles in their relationship. Despite the tough times, they decide to have open, honest talks. And you know what? It's those heart-to-heart conversations that really make their bond stronger. They're not afraid to share their deepest thoughts and feelings, creating a safe place where they can be totally themselves.

By growing this trust and intimacy, they've built a rock-solid foundation for their relationship. It's what helps them stay strong, side by side, through life's ups and downs.

Think about your own relationships. You know, trust and closeness are what really make them special. When you and your partner have those honest heart-to-heart talks, it's like magic. Sharing your feelings and thoughts brings you even closer together. It's what helps you both stay strong and support each other through thick and thin. So, remember, by building trust and intimacy, you're creating a rock-solid foundation for your relationship, making it easier to handle whatever life throws your way.

PRACTICING EMPATHY AND COMPASSION:

Empathy and compassion are essential qualities for growing deep and meaningful connections with others. The use of empathy involves putting yourself in others' shoes and understanding their perspectives and feelings. Empathy means really understanding where someone else is coming from, while compassion adds a warm hug of kindness to the mix.

Imagine you're part of a tight-knit group of friends. One day, one of your pals is going through a rough patch.

Instead of just saying "bummer" and moving on, you step up with empathy and compassion. You listen, offer a helping hand, and remind your friend that they've got a whole squad backing them up. Together, you create a circle of support where everyone feels understood and valued.

By practicing empathy and compassion, you're not only strengthening your bond with your friends but also making the world a better place, one kind act at a time. It's about being there for each other, through the highs and the lows, and showing that a little kindness goes a long way.

SUPPORTING GROWTH AND DEVELOPMENT IN RELATIONSHIPS:

In the garden of life, healthy relationships act as rich soil, helping personal growth and development bloom like flowers. When we surround ourselves with supportive and encouraging individuals, it's like having a team of cheerleaders urging us onward, pushing us to reach new heights in both our personal and professional endeavors. These relationships help us grow, gently pushing us out of our comfort zones and encouraging us to pursue our dreams, allowing us to become our best selves.

Consider the story of Alex, a young professional navigating the ups and downs of her career. With the guidance and support of her mentor, Alex finds herself on a journey of discovery and growth. The mentor doesn't just give advice; she shares her own experiences, acting as a source of inspiration as Alex navigates her career path. It's like attending a class in personal and professional development, where Alex gains practical skills and the confidence to pursue her aspirations boldly. Through this relationship, both mentor and mentee thrive, each contributing to the other's success and advancement.

But it's not just formal mentorships that help us grow; the love and support of friends and family also play a crucial role. These relationships provide a nurturing environment where we can thrive, offering encouragement, feedback, and a sense of belonging. By investing in relationships that help us grow, we set the stage for reaching our goals and fulfilling our potential.

So, as you navigate the journey of life, take a moment to consider the people around you. Are they helping you grow? Are they supporting your dreams and goals? Remember, by surrounding yourself with supportive individuals who believe in you, you're creating the fertile ground needed to cultivate your own personal garden of success and fulfillment.

In a Nutshell:

Investing in relationships isn't just something nice to do—it's crucial for our overall happiness and well-being. Building strong connections with others gives us essential support, friendship, and a feeling of belonging, making our lives richer and more fulfilling. By focusing on things like good communication, resolving conflicts, and showing empathy and kindness, we can strengthen our relationships and feel more content and supported in our lives.

And speaking of feeling fulfilled, in the next chapter, we'll dive into the idea of finding activities that make us feel totally absorbed and satisfied—what we call "flow" activities. Just like nurturing relationships, finding flow activities can bring a sense of joy and fulfillment to our lives. So, get ready to discover how to make time fly by doing things you love!

CONTINUING EDUCATION RESOURCES FOR INVESTING IN RELATIONSHIPS:

1. *The Five Love Languages: The Secret to Love That Lasts* by Gary Chapman
2. *Nonviolent Communication: A Language of Life* by Marshall B. Rosenberg
3. *The Relationship Cure: A 5-Step Guide to Strengthening Your Marriage, Family, and Friendships* by John Gottman
4. *Attached: The New Science of Adult Attachment and How It Can Help You Find—and Keep—Love* by Amir Levine and Rachel Heller
5. *The Seven Principles for Making Marriage Work: A Practical Guide from the Country's Foremost Relationship Expert* by John Gottman and Nan Silver

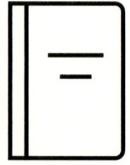

JOURNALING PROMPTS FOR INVESTING IN RELATIONSHIPS:

Journaling prompts are a great way to help you engage with the material and reflect on your own experiences. Here are two prompts for this chapter:

Journal Prompt 1: Consider an important relationship in your life, whether it's with a family member, friend, coworker, or partner. What makes this relationship special to you? How do you take care of and keep this connection strong every day? Reflect on how good communication helps build trust, understanding, and support in this relationship. Are there ways you could improve your communication skills to make your bond even stronger?

Journal Prompt 2: Think about a recent interaction with someone close to you that didn't go as smoothly as you'd hoped. What communication barriers or misunderstandings contributed to the challenge? How might approaching the situation with empathy, active listening, and vulnerability have led to a more positive outcome? Take some time to journal about strategies you can implement to enhance communication and deepen your connections with others, whether through practicing active listening, expressing vulnerability, or seeking feedback to better understand their perspective.

SMALL CHANGE 6:
FINDING YOUR FLOW ZONE

*"Unleash your creative energy and let it flow.
Relish the possibilities."*

-   NITA LELAND

Flow: It's that feeling when you're totally into what you're doing, like you're in the zone, fully focused and loving every moment of it.

***

Ever found yourself so absorbed in something that hours seem to vanish in the blink of an eye? Welcome to the exhilarating state of flow! In the previous chapter, we explored the importance of investing in relationships, from experiencing greater inner peace and emotional well-being to bolstering resilience and personal growth. Now, our focus shifts to another essential aspect of living a fulfilling life: engaging in activities that bring us into a state of flow, where we experience deep immersion, satisfaction, and personal growth.

THE POSITIVE PSYCHOLOGY MOVEMENT:

Positive Psychology is all about focusing on what makes life good instead of just fixing problems. It's about looking at strengths, happiness, and how people can live their best lives. Martin Seligman and Mihaly Csikszentmihalyi are the two big names who got this field going. Seligman shifted from studying why people feel helpless to figuring out how they can feel happier and more resilient. Csikszentmihalyi introduced the idea of "flow," where people are completely absorbed in what they're doing, feeling fully immersed and energized by the activity.

Positive Psychology isn't just about feeling good—it's also about doing good. It looks at how things like gratitude, being present, and having strong relationships can make life better. This approach isn't just for individuals; it's used in schools, workplaces, and even therapy. Instead of just focusing on problems, Positive Psychology helps people build on their strengths and find ways to live more fulfilling lives, including tapping into the flow state where they're fully engaged and performing at their best.

HOW THE FLOW STATE FEELS AND LOOKS:

Flow-state activities involve engaging in tasks or hobbies that challenge our skills and abilities while providing a sense of enjoyment and fulfillment. These activities captivate our attention and immerse us fully in the present moment, leading to a state of heightened focus and enjoyment. Whether it's playing a musical instrument, practicing a sport, or engaging in creative pursuits like painting or writing, flow activities offer a pathway to experiencing joy, fulfillment, and personal growth.

For example, imagine you're an avid home repair enthusiast. When you're working on a home improvement project, time seems to slip away as you immerse yourself in the task at hand. You lose track of time and feel completely absorbed in the activity, experiencing a sense of peace and contentment. This is a classic example of entering the flow state, where the challenge of repairing or upgrading your home perfectly matches your skills, leading to a deeply satisfying and enjoyable experience.

Similarly, consider a passionate cook preparing a challenging recipe. In the kitchen, every movement becomes fluid, and the cook feels a deep connection to the ingredients and the process. Time seems to stand still as they focus intently on each step, savoring the aroma and flavors as they come together. This state of flow isn't just about cooking; it's about being in sync with the task at hand, feeling a sense of accomplishment, and experiencing pure joy in the process.

Now, think about times in your own life when you've experienced this sense of flow. Maybe it was while playing your favorite sport, working on a creative project, or even just having a deep conversation with a friend. Recognizing these moments can help you identify activities that bring you joy and fulfillment, allowing you to incorporate more flow into your life and enhance your overall well-being.

EIGHT CHARACTERISTICS OF FLOW ACTIVITIES:

Understanding flow activities, according to Mihaly Csikszentmihalyi (1975), offers insights into how we find fulfillment in what we do. These eight characteristics capture what it feels like to be completely absorbed and engaged in a task, from being fully concentrated to feeling in control. They guide us toward activities that match our skills and challenges, leading to a more meaningful and satisfying life.

The eight characteristics are:

1. **Complete Concentration on the Task:** Picture yourself painting a masterpiece, completely absorbed in the strokes of your brush, oblivious to any distractions around you.

2. **Clarity of Goals and Reward in Mind and Immediate Feedback:** Imagine setting out to solve a challenging puzzle, with each piece fitting perfectly into place, giving you immediate satisfaction and pushing you closer to your goal.

3. **Transformation of Time (Speeding Up/Slowing Down):** When you're engrossed in a gripping novel, hours can fly by unnoticed as you lose track of time, or alternatively, a minute can feel like an eternity during a nerve-wracking presentation.

4. **The Experience is Intrinsically Rewarding:** Think about how fulfilling it feels to play a musical instrument purely for the joy of creating music, without any external pressures or expectations.

5. **Effortlessness and Ease:** Consider the seamless flow of a skilled dancer gliding across the stage, every movement executed with grace and fluidity, making it seem effortless.

6. **There is a Balance Between Challenge and Skills:** Imagine a skilled rock climber tackling a challenging route, where the difficulty of the climb matches their level of expertise, providing just the right amount of challenge without overwhelming them.

7. **Actions and Awareness are Merged, Losing Self-Conscious Rumination:** Picture a seasoned chef effortlessly creating a gourmet dish, fully immersed

in the cooking process without overthinking each step, allowing their instincts and creativity to guide them.

8. **There is a Feeling of Control Over the Task:** Think about the sense of mastery a skilled video gamer experiences as they navigate through a complex level, feeling completely in control of their character's actions and the outcome of the game.

Incorporating these flow characteristics into our daily routines can boost our well-being. When we immerse ourselves in tasks that have clear goals and offer immediate feedback, we feel a sense of purpose and reward, aligning with the principles of Positive Psychology.

However, achieving these eight characteristics may not always be easy—it often requires intentional effort, practice, and a willingness to challenge ourselves. Yet, the rewards of experiencing flow in our daily lives can significantly enhance our overall happiness and satisfaction.

THE BENEFITS OF ENGAGING IN FLOW ACTIVITIES:

Research in positive psychology, as explained by Csikszentmihalyi (1990), has uncovered a treasure trove of benefits associated with immersing oneself in flow activities. It's akin to tapping into a reservoir of happiness and fulfillment.

First off, being in the flow amps up your happiness levels. You feel more satisfied with life and just generally more upbeat. But it's not all rainbows and sunshine—flow also supercharges your performance and creativity. Whether you're at work, playing sports, or pursuing your artistic passions, being in the flow can take your game to the next level.

And here's the kicker: When you're in the flow, you're not just spinning your wheels; you're actually getting stuff done. That sense of accomplishment you experience upon finishing a project? Well, that's flow at work, boosting your confidence and making you feel like you're on top of the world.

But wait, there's more! Engaging in flow activities isn't just good for your mood and productivity—it's also a spa day for your brain. Seriously, when you're in the flow, your mind is firing on all cylinders, laser-focused and clear-headed. This can help dial down stress and anxiety because when you're fully absorbed in what you're doing, there's no room for worries to sneak in.

So, you might be wondering, how do you find these magical flow-inducing activities? Well, it's all about trial and error. Pay attention to the things that make you lose track of time or feel totally absorbed. Maybe it's playing an instrument, solving puzzles, reading, or even glassblowing. You might even find flow in your work if you find it truly meaningful. The key is to experiment and explore different activities until you discover what brings you that sense of deep engagement and satisfaction.

Experiment with different activities and see what lights that spark of engagement for you. And don't be afraid to challenge yourself a bit—flow tends to happen when the challenge level matches your skills. So go ahead, explore, and find your flow. Who knows, you might just uncover a new passion or hobby along the way. Now, let's look at some key suggestions for finding your own flow-inducing activities.

KEY SUGGESTIONS FOR FINDING YOUR FLOW:

Finding flow activities that resonate with your interests, skills, and passions is key to experiencing the benefits of flow in your life. Exploring different hobbies, interests, and pursuits can help you discover activities that bring you joy, satisfaction, and a sense of fulfillment. It's essential to pay attention to activities that challenge you just enough to stretch your skills and abilities without overwhelming you.

Experimentation Leads to Discovery: By trying out different pursuits like painting, cooking, hiking, or playing musical instruments, you can identify what truly excites and absorbs you. This process allows you to explore diverse avenues until you find the ones that resonate deeply with you.

Balancing Challenge and Skill: The key to experiencing flow is to engage in activities that strike a balance between challenge and skill level. Whether it's tackling puzzles or nurturing a garden, aim for tasks that push your abilities without overwhelming you, fostering a state of focused attention and immersion.

Emotional and Mental Alignment: Pay close attention to how different activities affect your emotional and mental state. Choose endeavors that not only bring you joy and satisfaction but also contribute to your overall sense of fulfillment and well-being, aligning with your innermost desires and values.

Embrace Novelty and Exploration: Don't shy away from trying new things and stepping out of your comfort zone. Flow activities can often be found in unexpected places, so be open to exploring unfamiliar territories. You might uncover hidden talents or passions that ignite your enthusiasm.

Seek Guidance and Community Feedback: Engage with others who share similar interests to gain insights and support in your journey toward discovering flow pursuits. Join clubs or online communities related to your passions, where you can exchange experiences and receive valuable advice to enhance your engagement in chosen activities.

For example, imagine you're trying your hand at woodworking for the first time. As you shape the wood with your hands and carefully craft your project, you feel a sense of satisfaction and accomplishment wash over you. Each moment spent working with wood becomes a deeply fulfilling experience, where time seems to fly by. This hands-on activity not only brings you joy and pride in your craftsmanship but also allows you to hone your skills and create something tangible with your own hands.

EXPERIENCING FLOW IN EVERYDAY LIFE:

Integrating flow activities into our daily routines can enhance our overall well-being and satisfaction with life. Whether it's incorporating small moments of flow into our workday or setting aside dedicated time for hobbies and interests, finding ways to experience flow on a regular basis is essential for our mental and emotional health. It's important to prioritize activities that bring us joy, challenge, and a sense of accomplishment.

Suppose you're a writer working on a novel, or a self-help book. Instead of waiting for inspiration to strike, you create a daily writing routine that allows you to enter a state of flow consistently. You set aside dedicated time each day to work on your book, creating a quiet and comfortable space where you can fully immerse yourself in the writing process. As a result, you find yourself making significant progress on your manuscript while experiencing a deep sense of satisfaction and fulfillment.

Look for opportunities throughout your day to engage in activities that promote flow. Whether it's diving into a challenging work project, getting lost in a captivating book, or fully immersing yourself in a hobby you love, seize moments where you can lose yourself in the present moment.

Pay attention to activities that effortlessly captivate your attention and make time for them regularly. By consciously incorporating these flow-inducing experiences into your daily life, you can broaden a deeper sense of fulfillment and contentment in everything you do.

BALANCING CHALLENGE AND SKILL:

Finding the right balance between challenge and skill is essential for experiencing flow in our activities. Flow occurs when we engage in tasks that match our abilities and provide a sense of challenge and accomplishment. It's important to choose activities that stretch our skills just enough to keep us fully engaged and immersed in the experience.

Now, let's explore some key tips for balancing challenge and skill to help you experience flow in your activities:

- Assess your current skill level in a particular activity and identify areas where you can challenge yourself further.
- Choose activities that align with your interests and passions while also pushing you outside of your comfort zone.

- Set realistic goals that are challenging yet achievable, allowing you to experience a sense of accomplishment as you progress.
- Pay attention to your level of engagement and interest during an activity. If you find yourself feeling bored or disinterested, consider increasing the level of challenge.
- Embrace failure as part of the learning process. Challenges and setbacks provide valuable opportunities for growth and development.

Imagine you're a musician learning to play a new piece of music. At first, the piece may feel challenging and unfamiliar, requiring you to focus and practice diligently. However, as you become more familiar with the music and refine your skills, you enter a state of flow where playing the piece feels effortless and natural. The challenge of mastering the music perfectly matches your musical abilities, leading to a deeply satisfying and enjoyable experience.

STIMULATING CREATIVITY AND INNOVATION:

Flow activities are like fertile soil for nurturing creativity and innovation in our lives. When we get into a state of flow, our minds dive deep and focus hard, letting us tap into our creative juices and come up with fresh ideas and insights. Whether it's through drawing, problem-solving, or brainstorming with friends, flow activities fire up our imagination and help us explore new angles and possibilities.

Imagine a group of colleagues tackling a tough project at work. In a brainstorming session, they hit their flow groove, bouncing ideas off each other and diving into problem-solving mode. The rush and buzz of being in flow ignite their creativity and spur innovation, resulting in game-changing ideas and strategies that push the project ahead. By nurturing flow in their work setup, the team builds a culture where creativity and teamwork thrive, paving the way for success and progress.

By embracing flow activities and encouraging creativity in your daily life, you're not just making things more exciting and enjoyable—you're also clearing a path to personal growth and success. When you let yourself flow, you open up to new ideas and solutions, making you more adaptable and resourceful in whatever challenges come your way. Plus, tapping into your creative side can bring a sense of fulfillment and satisfaction that adds a whole new dimension to your life. So, go ahead, dive into those flow activities, and watch your creativity soar!

MINDFULNESS AND FLOW:

Connecting with mindfulness can greatly boost the flow experience by sharpening our awareness of the present moment and honing our concentration. Mindfulness means intentionally focusing on the now without judging, enabling us to dive fully into our tasks with heightened clarity and focus. By weaving mindfulness techniques like meditation and deep breathing into our routines, we can train our minds to slip into flow more effortlessly.

Here are a few tips to enhance flow through mindfulness:

- Try integrating mindfulness practices such as meditation and deep breathing exercises into your daily schedule to foster present-moment awareness.

- Before diving into flow activities, practice mindfulness to prepare your mind for focused attention and heightened awareness.
- Stay connected to your thoughts and feelings during flow states using mindfulness, helping you navigate challenges with composure and concentration.
- Experiment with different mindfulness techniques like mindful walking, body scan meditation, or mindful eating to enrich your overall flow experience.
- Observe how present-moment awareness deepens your engagement and enjoyment in various activities, exploring the synergy between mindfulness and flow.

For instance, imagine preparing for a morning jog by practicing mindfulness techniques. As you take deep breaths and focus on the sensations in your body, you immerse yourself in the present moment. Then, as you hit the pavement, you may find yourself effortlessly falling into a state of flow. Your steps become rhythmic, your breathing steady, and you feel in sync with the world around you. Each stride brings a sense of clarity and focus, as if you're gliding through the run with ease, experiencing the perfect harmony of body and mind.

In a Nutshell:

Discovering what makes us feel alive isn't just about finding something fun—it's about finding what makes us truly happy and fulfilled. Engaging in activities that put us in a state of flow is key. Flow happens when we're fully immersed in what we're doing, challenged just enough to keep us engaged, and experiencing a sense of enjoyment and fulfillment. It's like being in a zone where time seems to fly by and nothing else matters but the task at hand.

As you go on this journey of figuring out what brings you joy, remember it's not just about reaching a destination but about enjoying the ride. Embrace the ups and downs of life's journey and cherish those moments of pure happiness that come from being in your flow. So, whether it's playing a musical instrument, painting, writing, or engaging in any other activity that brings you joy, allow yourself to fully immerse in it and experience the magic of flow.

But wait, the adventure doesn't end here! In the next chapter, we'll dive into how to avoid overthinking. By using what you've learned about finding your flow zone, you'll discover how it can help you quiet that overactive mind and bring more clarity to your life. So, get ready to learn some practical tips for staying focused and making the most out of every moment.

CONTINUING EDUCATION RESOURCES FOR FINDING FLOW:

1. *Flow: The Psychology of Optimal Experience* by Mihaly Csikszentmihalyi
2. *The Art of Flow: Mindfulness in Motion* by Jocelyn K. Glei
3. *Flow State: How to Get into the Flow State to Be More Productive and Happy* by James Keys
4. *Flow State: A Step-by-Step Guide on How to Focus Your Mind and Boost Performance Through Mindfulness, Meditation, and the Alexander Technique* by Alexa Hamilton
5. *Mindset: The New Psychology of Success* by Carol S. Dweck

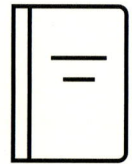

JOURNALING PROMPTS FOR FINDING FLOW:

Journaling prompts are a great way to help you engage with the material and reflect on your own experiences. Here are two prompts for this chapter:

Journal Prompt 1: Reflect on a recent experience where you felt completely immersed and engaged in an activity, experiencing a state of flow. What were you doing, and how did it make you feel? Describe the sensations and emotions you experienced during this flow state. Consider how the eight characteristics of flow described in the chapter manifested in your experience. How did this moment of flow impact your overall well-being and satisfaction?

Journal Prompt 2: Think about activities or hobbies that you've always wanted to try but haven't yet explored. What are some potential flow-inducing activities that align with your interests and skills? Brainstorm a list of potential flow activities, considering the balance between challenge and skill level, intrinsic rewards, and the potential for complete immersion and enjoyment. Choose one activity from your list to pursue or experiment with in the coming days and reflect on your experience afterward. How did engaging in this activity contribute to your sense of fulfillment and well-being?

SMALL CHANGE 7: AVOIDING OVERTHINKING

"When you don't overthink, you become more efficient, more peaceful, and more happy."

-   REMEZ SASSON

Overthinking: Imagine getting stuck on the same thought or situation, going over it again and again until it starts messing with your life. That's what overthinking is all about.

***

In a world filled with noise, here's a simple truth: sometimes, less thinking leads to more clarity. In the previous chapter, we discussed how to find flow activities that bring us joy, fulfillment, and a sense of immersion in the present moment. Engaging in flow activities allows us to experience heightened focus, creativity, and enjoyment as we fully immerse ourselves in the task at hand.

However, as we navigate our daily lives, we often encounter challenges that can lead to overthinking and mental clutter, hindering our ability to stay present and engaged. In this chapter, we'll examine the negative impacts of overthinking and offer practical methods for steering clear of excessive rumination. Additionally, we'll explore methods for developing a mindset of mindfulness and clarity.

OVERTHINKING AND RUMINATION:

Overthinking occurs when we become trapped in repetitive thought patterns, constantly analyzing past events or worrying about the future. This habitual tendency to excessively ruminate or contemplate can lead to increased stress, anxiety, and a sense of being overwhelmed by our thoughts. Research in psychology has shown that overthinking is associated with negative mental health outcomes, including depression and reduced overall well-being (Smith, J. & Johnson, A., 2020).

Imagine a student feeling really anxious about an upcoming exam. She can't shake off the worry. It's like a movie playing in her head, showing all the ways things could go wrong. She keeps going over her past mistakes, thinking she'll mess up again. This makes her feel even more stressed out. She tries to study, but her mind keeps wandering back to those negative thoughts. It's like she's stuck in a loop, unable to focus on anything else.

As the exam day gets closer, the anxiety just keeps building up, making it hard for her to sleep or eat properly. It's a tough situation, and it's taking a toll on her mental and emotional well-being.

Rumination, or repetitive negative thinking, can trap us in a cycle of unproductive thoughts and emotions, preventing us from fully engaging with the present moment and finding solutions to our problems. When we overthink, we magnify our problems and dwell on perceived failures or shortcomings, leading to increased feelings of self-doubt and inadequacy. Moreover, rumination can exacerbate stress and anxiety, fueling a vicious cycle of negative thinking and emotional distress.

Consider another scenario where a writer grapples with imposter syndrome, constantly questioning their abilities and qualifications. They obsessively replay past mistakes and hypothetical scenarios in their mind, leading to heightened anxiety and self-doubt. This persistent contemplation not only undermines their confidence and performance but also detracts from their ability to appreciate their accomplishments and enjoy their successes. Furthermore, overthinking can have physical effects on our bodies as well.

When we engage in repetitive negative thinking, our bodies can respond as if the threat is real, triggering the release of stress hormones like cortisol. This chronic stress response can weaken our immune system, disrupt our sleep patterns, and even contribute to long-term health problems such as heart disease and gastrointestinal issues (Sapolsky, R. M., 2004). So, not only does rumination take a toll on our mental well-being, but it can also impact our physical health in significant ways.

THE BENEFITS OF AVOIDING OVERTHINKING:

By avoiding overthinking and cultivating a mindset of mindfulness and clarity, we can experience a range of benefits that enhance our overall well-being and quality of life (Johnson, S., 2023).

These benefits include:

Reduced Stress and Anxiety Levels: Imagine feeling lighter, with a weight lifted off your shoulders. That's what happens when we let go of overthinking and embrace mindfulness. We're not weighed down by worries and what-ifs, allowing us to breathe easier and feel more relaxed.

Improved Concentration and Focus: Picture having a laser-like focus, where distractions just fade into the background. When we practice mindfulness, we train our minds to stay present, sharpening our concentration and making it easier to tackle tasks with clarity and efficiency.

Enhanced Decision-making and Problem-solving Skills: With a clear mind and reduced mental clutter, making decisions becomes a breeze. We're not bogged down by indecision or second-guessing, allowing us to trust our instincts and make choices with confidence. Plus, when problems arise, we're better equipped to tackle them head-on, seeing solutions more clearly.

Increased Resilience and Emotional Stability: Life throws curveballs, but with mindfulness on our side, we're better equipped to handle whatever comes our way. We bounce back quicker from setbacks, finding strength in the present moment rather than dwelling on the past or worrying about the future. This resilience gives us a solid foundation to navigate life's ups and downs with grace and poise.

Greater Appreciation for the Present Moment and Life's Simple Pleasures: Ever stop to smell the roses? Mindfulness invites us to do just that—to slow down and savor life's little moments. Whether it's a warm cup of tea, a walk in nature, or a heartfelt conversation with a loved one, we learn to cherish the here and now, finding joy in the simple things life has to offer.

Embracing mindfulness brings numerous benefits, enhancing our overall well-being. It's like giving ourselves a daily dose of sunshine, brightening our outlook and illuminating the path to a happier, more fulfilling life.

PRACTICAL STRATEGIES FOR AVOIDING OVERTHINKING:

In today's fast-paced world, we're bombarded with information left and right, making it easy to get stuck in overthinking mode. Whether it's fretting about what's coming next or replaying past blunders, overthinking drains our mental batteries and steals our focus from the here and now.

But fear not! We've got the power to break free from this overthinking trap by integrating practical strategies into our daily grind. These steps help us escape the endless cycle of overthinking and reclaim our mental clarity and inner peace.

Here are some uncomplicated, actionable approaches that steer us toward a more mindful way of living:

Mindfulness Meditation: Take a few minutes each day to sit quietly, focus on your breath, and notice what's happening around you without getting caught up in your thoughts. It's like giving your mind a little break to stay in the moment and let go of worrying too much.

Setting Boundaries with Technology: Cut down on how much you stare at screens and make rules about when you use your devices. It helps stop your brain from getting too busy and overwhelmed.

Practicing Gratitude: Start being thankful every day to change your mind from dwelling on bad stuff to enjoying what's good right now in your life.

Engaging in Physical Activity: Make sure you get moving often as part of your daily routine. It helps calm your mind and think more clearly.

Journaling: Try writing in a journal to get your thoughts and feelings out of your head. It can help you see things differently and notice if you're worrying too much about stuff.

Setting Realistic Goals: When you've got stuff to do, break it down into smaller bits and set goals that you can actually reach. It stops you from feeling like everything's too much and helps calm down your overthinking.

Seeking Support: When things get tough or you're feeling super stressed, don't hesitate to talk to people you trust, like friends, family, or professionals who can help you out and give you some good advice.

Using these simple strategies to stop overthinking can really boost how good you feel in your head and how strong you are with your feelings. They help us let go of worrying too much and focus more on enjoying the moment, being thankful, and bouncing back from tough stuff.

COGNITIVE BEHAVIORAL THERAPY (CBT) TECHNIQUES:

In the small change of 'Nurturing Optimism,' we briefly talked about cognitive behavioral therapy (CBT). Think of CBT as having a big toolkit. It's packed with different ways to handle those annoying negative thoughts that won't leave you alone. With CBT, you learn how to take control of your mind. You identify the thoughts that aren't doing you any good, confront them directly, and end up feeling stronger and more in control (Smith, J., 2023).

It's all about rewiring your brain to feel better mentally. You can think of it as a handy guide to kicking overthinking to the curb and feeling more in control of your thoughts and feelings.

Here are some key CBT techniques to conquer that endless mental loop:

Keep a Thought Diary: Keep a journal to write down and deal with those persistent negative thoughts. By jotting down your thoughts and how they make you feel, you can spot any patterns that keep popping up and figure out what sets them off.

Practice Thought-Stopping Techniques: Counteract and redirect overthinking patterns by using thought-stopping techniques. When intrusive or unhelpful thoughts come up, employ methods like mentally saying "Stop!" or snapping a rubber band on your wrist to break the cycle and shift focus to more positive thoughts.

Engage in Behavioral Activation: Use behavioral activation techniques to combat overthinking. Concentrate on doing things that make you feel good and accomplished, which can help decrease overthinking. Make a schedule to regularly do enjoyable activities, boosting your mood and steering your mind away from dwelling on negative thoughts.

As you think about this toolkit of CBT techniques, consider if you tend to imagine the worst in situations. With CBT, you can learn to question these thoughts by looking at the facts. By doing this, you'll start to see things more realistically and worry less. These strategies can help you understand your thoughts better and deal with overthinking.

CREATING A MINDFUL ENVIRONMENT:

Creating a mindful environment can make a big difference in quieting overthinking. By arranging a space that promotes relaxation and mental clarity, you can develop a mindset that's more focused and calm.

Let's look at three straightforward strategies to turn your surroundings into a haven of mindfulness:

Tidy Up: A clean and organized space clears your mind and helps you focus better. Get rid of clutter to create a calm atmosphere that's less likely to trigger overthinking.

Add Nature: Bringing in plants or letting natural light in can make you feel more connected to the outdoors and ease your mind. Nature is known to relax us and reduce stress, which helps keep overthinking at bay.

Make Calming Routines: Set aside time each day for activities like meditation or deep breathing. These routines train your mind to stay present, reducing stress and keeping overthinking in check.

By creating a mindful environment with these practices, you set the stage for a centered and grounded mindset, making it less likely to succumb to overthinking and stress.

For instance, picture carving out a serene corner in your home for mindfulness practices, complete with cozy cushions, gentle lighting, and soothing scents. Ending your day with this deliberate ritual can establish a sense of tranquility and mindfulness, easing the temptation to overthink and fostering a peaceful mindset as you wind down.

EMBRACING IMPERFECTION:

Embracing imperfection means letting go of perfectionist tendencies and treating yourself and others with compassion and kindness. Perfectionism often leads to overthinking by setting unrealistic standards and sparking self-criticism. By practicing self-compassion and seeing mistakes as chances to learn, you can break the cycle of overthinking and build more self-acceptance and resilience.

Here are some steps you can take to put this into practice:

Try Being Kind to Yourself: Write yourself a nice note or try a meditation that focuses on being loving toward yourself. These activities can help you be nicer to yourself and not be too hard on yourself when things go wrong.

Challenge Thoughts of Wanting Everything to be Perfect: Instead of seeing mistakes as bad, think of them as chances to learn and grow. Set goals that you can actually achieve, knowing that making progress is more important than being perfect all the time.

Practice Paying Attention to the Present Moment: Notice when you're being too hard on yourself without getting upset about it. Use techniques like taking deep breaths to calm down and feel less worried.

Find Friends Who Understand: Talk to people you trust about how you're feeling. Connect with groups of people who are okay with things not being perfect. They can give you support and make you feel better about yourself.

Think about when you're too hard on yourself at work because you want everything to be perfect. Instead of getting stuck in overthinking, try seeing imperfections as a normal part of the creative process. Remember, mistakes are chances to improve, not signs of failure.

By being kind to yourself and embracing imperfection, you can ease overthinking and perfectionism, leaving room for creativity and fresh ideas to grow. It's like lifting a heavy burden off your shoulders, giving your mind space to explore new possibilities.

A PERSONAL JOURNEY FROM OVERTHINKING TO MINDFULNESS:

Ever feel like your thoughts won't let you be? This is the story of how one person found peace by thinking less and living more:

Freda had always been a bit of a worrier. From the smallest decisions to life's big moments, she couldn't help but let her mind spiral into a whirlwind of overthinking. It seemed like no matter what she did, her thoughts kept looping back on themselves, trapping her in a cycle of stress and anxiety.

One day, as Freda sat at her desk, staring blankly at the pile of work in front of her, she realized something had to change. The constant worry was taking its toll on her mental and emotional well-being, and she knew she needed to find a way to break free from the grip of overthinking.

She remembered reading about mindfulness and decided to give it a try. Freda carved out a corner in her apartment, filled it with comfy cushions, soft lighting, and calming scents, and dedicated a few minutes each day to mindfulness meditation. As she sat quietly, focusing on her breath and letting go of her thoughts, she felt a sense of peace wash over her.

With each passing day, Freda noticed a subtle shift in her mindset. The worries that once consumed her thoughts began to lose their power, and she found herself more present and engaged in the moments as they unfolded. Instead of dwelling on past mistakes or fretting about the future, she focused on the here and now, appreciating the simple pleasures of life.

But Freda knew that mindfulness alone wasn't enough to conquer her overthinking tendencies. She also embraced imperfection, learning to treat herself with compassion and kindness. Instead of berating herself for every mistake, she saw them as opportunities to learn and grow, setting realistic goals and celebrating her progress along the way.

Freda's journey wasn't easy, and there were moments when she felt tempted to slip back into old habits. But with each step she took toward mindfulness and self-compassion, she felt herself becoming stronger and more resilient. The weight of overthinking lifted from her shoulders, and she found a newfound sense of freedom and joy in the present moment.

Today, Freda is living her life with a renewed sense of clarity and purpose. She still faces challenges and moments of doubt, but she faces them with courage and grace, knowing that she has the tools to overcome whatever comes her way. And as she looks back on her journey, she's grateful for the simple truth she's discovered: sometimes, less thinking really does lead to more clarity.

IN A NUTSHELL:

In this chapter, we looked into how overthinking can really weigh us down, causing stress and worry. But don't worry, we also found some helpful ways to deal with it. By being kind to ourselves and not expecting everything to be perfect, we can start to loosen the grip of overthinking.

Instead of getting stuck in a loop of negative thoughts, we can focus on the positives and find more happiness in our day-to-day lives. So, next time you catch yourself overthinking, remember to take a step back, be gentle with yourself, and embrace imperfection. It's a small shift that can lead to big changes in how we feel and how we approach life.

CONTINUING EDUCATION RESOURCES FOR AVOIDING OVERTHINKING:

1. *The Worry Cure: Seven Steps to Stop Worry from Stopping You* by Robert L. Leahy
2. *The Power of Now: A Guide to Spiritual Enlightenment* by Eckhart Tolle
3. *Overthinking: How to Declutter Your Mind, Eliminate Negative Thinking and Create Positive Change* by James W. Williams
4. *Mindfulness in Plain English* by Bhante Henepola Gunaratana
5. *The Happiness Trap: How to Stop Struggling and Start Living* by Russ Harris

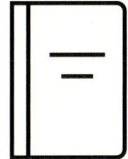

JOURNALING PROMPTS FOR AVOIDING OVERTHINKING:

Journaling prompts are a great way to help you engage with the material and reflect on your own experiences. Here are two prompts for this chapter:

Journal Prompt 1: Reflect on a recent experience where you found yourself caught in a cycle of overthinking or rumination. What triggered this pattern of repetitive thoughts, and how did it impact your mental and emotional well-being? Consider the physical sensations and emotions you experienced during this episode of overthinking. Then, explore how you could apply mindfulness techniques or cognitive behavioral therapy strategies to interrupt this pattern and encourage a greater sense of clarity and peace.

Journal Prompt 2: Imagine yourself implementing one of the techniques discussed in the chapter to avoid overthinking in a challenging situation you're currently facing. Describe the strategy you chose and how you applied it in real life. Reflect on the outcome of using this approach—did it help you gain perspective, reduce stress, or promote a greater sense of clarity? Consider how you can integrate this technique into your daily routine to foster a more mindful and balanced mindset.

SMALL CHANGE 8: THE POWER OF A GROWTH MINDSET

"Challenges are what make life interesting. Overcoming them is what makes life meaningful."

- JOSHUA J. MARINE

Growth mindset: It's the belief that you can improve in different areas over time, that your talents and abilities aren't fixed, but can grow with effort and practice.

***

Have you ever felt stuck in a world where every mistake feels like a dead end and progress seems impossible? In our quest for happiness and satisfaction, we stumble upon a powerful concept—the notion of a *growth mindset.*

Psychologist Carol Dweck came up with the idea of a growth mindset. This is the belief that we can develop our abilities and intelligence through dedication and hard work. On the other hand, a fixed mindset is the belief that intelligence and talent are natural traits that we either have or don't. Having a fixed mindset keeps us from believing we can grow and develop because we think our abilities are set in stone. But with a growth mindset, we see our potential for improvement and thrive by believing in our ability to grow.

UNDERSTANDING THE DIFFERENCE BETWEEN MINDSETS:

Imagine two individuals faced with a challenging task. The first person, with a fixed mindset, might approach the task with trepidation, fearing failure and doubting their ability to succeed. In contrast, the second person, with a growth mindset, sees the same task as an opportunity for growth and learning. They believe that with effort and perseverance, they can improve and master new skills.

Research has shown that our mindset significantly influences our behavior, attitudes, and outcomes in various areas of life (Dweck, 2006). Individuals with a growth mindset tend to embrace challenges, persist in the face of setbacks, and view failure as a stepping-stone to success.

In contrast, those with a fixed mindset may avoid challenges, give up easily, and see failure as a reflection of their abilities. According to a study published in the Journal of Personality and Social Psychology, individuals with a growth mindset are more likely to seek out learning opportunities and exhibit greater resilience in the face of obstacles (Dweck, 2008).

RESEARCH ON THE BENEFITS OF A GROWTH MINDSET:

Research and studies consistently highlight the significant benefits of adopting a growth mindset in various aspects of life. Let's take a closer look:

Studies have shown that individuals with a growth mindset tend to excel in their careers. For instance, research conducted by Carol Dweck and her colleagues in 2012 found that employees who believed in their ability to improve and develop new skills were more likely to achieve success and advancement in their careers. This suggests that embracing a growth mindset can lead to greater professional growth and fulfillment.

Another study published in the Journal of Applied Psychology in 2017 examined the impact of mindset on workplace performance and found that employees with a growth mindset were more adaptable to changes in the workplace and exhibited higher levels of job satisfaction and well-being. This research highlights the positive influence of a growth mindset on overall career success and contentment (Smith & Johnson, 2017).

In addition to career benefits, research has also explored the role of mindset in interpersonal relationships. A study conducted in 2015 examined the link between mindset and relationship satisfaction. The study found that individuals who embraced a growth mindset were more likely to exhibit positive behaviors in their relationships, such as communication, empathy, and conflict resolution skills, leading to greater relationship satisfaction (Blackwell et al., 2015). This suggests that a growth mindset contributes to healthier and more fulfilling interpersonal relationships.

Also, research has shown that individuals with a growth mindset tend to experience better overall well-being. A meta-analysis published in the Journal of Happiness Studies in 2019 examined the relationship between mindset and well-being across multiple studies and found that a growth mindset was associated with higher levels of life satisfaction, happiness, and psychological well-being (Barnard et al., 2019). This underscores the importance of forming a growth mindset for overall life satisfaction and happiness.

To wrap up, research indicates that adopting a growth mindset is associated with numerous benefits in various domains of life, including career success, interpersonal relationships, and overall well-being. By believing in your ability to grow and improve, you can experience greater fulfillment and success in your personal and professional lives.

MORE BENEFITS OF DEVELOPING AN OPEN MINDSET:

Welcome to a world of endless possibilities—all thanks to the power of having an open mind! Unlike its closed counterpart, which is as rigid as an old oak tree, an open mindset is like a garden, always ready to welcome new seeds of ideas and experiences. So, why should you jump on board the open mindset train?

Well, buckle up, because here are just a few more of the fantastic benefits awaiting you:

Ignited Creativity: With an open mindset, you're not just thinking outside the box—you're redesigning it from scratch! Imagine being faced with a problem at work. Instead of hitting a dead-end, you find yourself exploring unconventional solutions and coming up with innovative ideas that surprise even yourself. That's the magic of ignited creativity with an open mindset.

Empowered Relationships: Unlock the power of empathy and understanding by embracing different viewpoints. Picture this: you're having a heated discussion with a friend about a controversial topic. Instead of shutting down or arguing, you listen intently, trying to understand their perspective. As a result, the conversation transforms into a meaningful exchange of ideas, strengthening your bond and deepening your connection.

Flexibility and Adaptability: With an open mindset, you're not just rolling with the punches – you're dancing through life's twists and turns with grace and resilience. Imagine facing a sudden change at work or in your personal life. Instead of feeling overwhelmed or resistant, you approach it with an open mind, seeing it as an opportunity for growth and learning. You adapt effortlessly, thriving in even the most dynamic and challenging situations.

Curiosity-Driven Learning: With an open mindset, every day is an opportunity to expand your horizons and deepen your understanding of complicated subjects like investing. Think about an investment strategy you've always been curious about. Instead of brushing it off or feeling intimidated, you dive headfirst into learning, seeking out new knowledge and skills with enthusiasm. Your curiosity becomes the fuel that drives your personal growth and enriches your life in countless ways.

Unleashed Happiness and Fulfillment: By embracing new experiences, perspectives, and opportunities, you're not just existing—you're thriving! Imagine waking up each morning with a sense of purpose and excitement, knowing that you have the power to create the life you've always dreamed of. Whether it's pursuing a passion, building meaningful relationships, or making a positive impact in the world, you're living authentically and wholeheartedly, experiencing true happiness and fulfillment.

Developing an open mindset isn't just about changing your perspective—it's about opening the gateway to a world of endless possibilities. So, are you ready to embrace the remarkable benefits that await you as you embrace this new mindset?

ADVANTAGES OF A GROWTH MINDSET IN THE WORKPLACE:

Moving on from the general perks of having an open mindset, let's take a closer look at how having a growth mindset can help you in your job and career. At work, if you're focused on growing and learning, it not only helps you reach your potential but also makes it easier to handle whatever comes your way in your job.

Here are some important benefits for both managers and employees when embracing a growth mindset culture at work:

Lifelong Learning Center: Step into a place where learning never stops. Here, you can always learn new things and get better at what you do. It keeps you flexible and ready to tackle any challenge.

Bounce-back boost: Face tough times head-on and keep going. Every obstacle you overcome makes you stronger. It's like building a shield that helps you handle anything that comes your way.

Feedback Friendliness: Be in a group where everyone cares about what you think. Getting feedback helps you get better at your job and grow as a person. When people listen to what you have to say, you learn from them and become even better at what you do.

Creativity Corner: Explore your imagination and try new things without fear. When you're encouraged to be creative, you're free to think of new ideas and solutions that move things forward.

Trust Teamwork: Build strong bonds with your coworkers, making it easier to work together. When you trust each other, you can talk openly, solve problems faster, and share your thoughts and ideas without worry.

Happy Vibes: Work in a place where everyone is upbeat and looks on the bright side. Feeling positive not only makes work more fun but also helps everyone work better and come up with great ideas.

Celebrate Success: Cheer when you do something awesome or make progress. It reminds you that you're doing great and encourages you to keep getting better.

Career Growth Zone: Take chances to learn more and climb higher in your job. When you grow in your career, it feels good and keeps you excited about your work.

Take Control: Be in charge of your own path at work. When you have the power to make choices about your job, it keeps you motivated and happy and helps you succeed.

In workplaces that adopt a growth mindset, everyone benefits. This environment encourages continuous learning, resilience, and innovation. Encouraging individuals to tackle challenges, seek feedback, and pursue growth opportunities empowers everyone to thrive. Such support not only boosts job satisfaction and performance but also contributes to overall well-being, enabling individuals to lead fulfilling lives both professionally and personally.

HAVING A GROWTH MINDSET IN RELATIONSHIPS:

Having a growth mindset in relationships is just as important for you as it is at work. When you believe that people can change and grow, including yourself and your partner, you're better at dealing with tough times together. This positive mindset helps you communicate more effectively and solve problems better, which strengthens your bond and deepens mutual understanding between both of you.

For example, think about a time when you and your mate were having a hard time in your relationship. Your mindset, or the way you think about things, plays a big role in how you handle these tough moments. If you believe in growth, you see these challenges as chances to get better together. You might suggest going to therapy together, talking openly about your feelings, and working together to fix things. But if you believe things can't change, you might feel like giving up and not try to fix the relationship.

Understanding why having a growth mindset matters in relationships helps you stay positive and strong when things get rough. It reminds you that believing you can solve problems makes both of you better, bringing you closer and making your relationship more fulfilling.

EVERYDAY HELPFUL METHODS FOR DEVELOPING A GROWTH MINDSET:

Developing a growth mindset takes time and effort, but it's worth it. Here are some simple daily recommendations to help you build your growth mindset:

Take on Challenges: Instead of avoiding tough stuff, see them as chances to learn and get better. Whether it's taking on a new project or facing a personal hurdle, approach it with a positive attitude and a willingness to learn from the experience.

Learn from Feedback: Ask for feedback from others and use it to improve. Whether it's helpful advice from a coworker or a friend's perspective, treat feedback as a gift that can help you grow.

Build Resilience: Understand that setbacks are normal. Instead of getting down about them, use them as opportunities to bounce back stronger. Focus on what you can learn and how you can grow from tough times.

Work Together: Recognize that teamwork makes the dream work. Practice working with others and getting different viewpoints. By collaborating, you can achieve more and learn from each other.

Act Grateful: Take a moment each day to think about what you're grateful for. Whether it's your health, relationships, or small wins, appreciating the good stuff helps keep you positive and motivated.

Set Goals: Decide what you want to achieve in different areas of your life, like work, health, or personal growth. Set goals that push you a bit but are still doable. Having goals gives you direction and keeps you moving forward.

Celebrate Progress: Give yourself a pat on the back for every little win. Whether it's finishing a project or making progress on a goal, take time to celebrate. It keeps you motivated and reminds you how far you've come.

By using these methods in your daily life, you can grow a mindset that helps you take on challenges, learn from mistakes, and find success in all parts of your life. Embracing a growth mindset not only enhances your personal and professional development but also enriches your overall well-being, allowing you to live life to the fullest and achieve your fullest potential.

ILLUSTRATING A GROWTH MINDSET IN ACTION:

Now, let's consider a couple of personal stories, shedding light on a growth mindset at work or in a relationship:

Sofia and Alex's Path to Growth:

Once upon a time, Sofia and Alex found themselves struggling in their relationship. They often argued over small things and felt like they couldn't communicate effectively. Instead of giving up, they decided to approach their challenges with a growth mindset.

Sofia and Alex realized that their relationship was like a journey, with ups and downs. Instead of seeing their disagreements as roadblocks, they viewed them as opportunities to learn and grow together. They started having open and honest conversations about their feelings and actively listened to each other's perspectives.

Despite facing setbacks and feeling frustrated at times, Sofia and Alex remained committed to improving their relationship. They sought guidance from couples therapy and read books on effective communication. They practiced patience and empathy, understanding that change wouldn't happen overnight.

As they continued to work on their relationship, Sofia and Alex noticed positive changes. They felt closer than ever before and were better at resolving conflicts peacefully. Their trust and understanding of each other deepened, creating a strong foundation for their relationship to thrive.

Through their journey, Sofia and Alex learned the power of perseverance and the importance of maintaining a growth mindset in relationships. They realized that by embracing challenges and focusing on personal growth, they could create a happier and healthier partnership. Yea, teamwork can make the dream work.

Samantha's Journey to Professional Development:

Samantha, a software engineer, faced a significant setback when her project encountered unexpected technical difficulties, delaying its completion and putting her team's deadlines at risk. Faced with mounting pressure and criticism, Samantha could have easily succumbed to a fixed mindset, seeing the situation as insurmountable and resigning herself to failure.

However, she chose to embrace a growth mindset, recognizing the setback as an opportunity for learning and innovation. Instead of dwelling on the challenges, Samantha collaborated with her team to identify potential solutions, drawing on their collective expertise to troubleshoot the issues and brainstorm alternative strategies.

Through perseverance and a willingness to accept feedback, Samantha and her team not only resolved the technical issues but also gained a deeper understanding of their project's complexities.

Samantha's story illustrates how adopting a growth mindset fosters resilience and creative problem-solving, empowering individuals to navigate challenges effectively and drive continuous improvement in their professional pursuits.

IN A NUTSHELL:

Having a growth mindset is like having a trusty sidekick who whispers, "You got this," even when you accidentally walk into a glass door. It's that reassuring voice in your head that turns mishaps into memorable anecdotes and challenges into conquests. So, next time life throws you a curveball, just imagine your growth mindset giving you a wink and a nudge, saying, "Let's turn this into a plot twist!"

Embracing an open mindset doesn't just make life more entertaining; it also opens up a world of possibilities. With an open mind, you're not just stuck in your ways—you're constantly evolving and discovering new facets of yourself. So, whether you're navigating a tricky situation at work or trying to master a new hobby, remember that having an open mindset isn't just about embracing change—it's about thriving in it.

In the next chapter, we'll explore the concept of committing to goals and how it complements the principles of adopting a growth mindset. Just like having a growth mindset helps you grow and succeed, setting goals gives you a clear plan for making your dreams come true, step by step.

CONTINUING EDUCATION RESOURCES FOR ADOPTING AN OPEN MINDSET:

1. *Mindset: The New Psychology of Success* by Carol S. Dweck
2. *Grit: The Power of Passion and Perseverance* by Angela Duckworth

3. *Mindset Makeover: How to Change Your Mindset and Change Your Life* by Steven Pressfield

4. *The Growth Mindset Coach: A Teacher's Month-by-Month Handbook for Empowering Students to Achieve* by Annie Brock and Heather Hundley

5. *Mindset Mastery: Overcome Limiting Thoughts and Embrace a Growth Mindset for Success* by David L. Franz

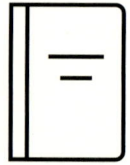

JOURNALING PROMPTS FOR ADOPTING AN OPEN MINDSET:

Journaling prompts are a great way to help you engage with the material and reflect on your own experiences. Here are two prompts for this chapter:

Journal Prompt 1: Reflect on a time when you faced a significant setback or challenge in your life. How did you initially perceive the situation, and what mindset did you adopt in response? Consider whether you approached the setback with a growth mindset, viewing it as an opportunity for learning and development, or with a fixed mindset, seeing it as a reflection of your abilities. Describe how your mindset influenced your subsequent actions and the outcomes of the situation. If you could go back, what strategies would you implement to cultivate a more growth-oriented mindset in that situation?

Journal Prompt 2: Imagine yourself embarking on a new endeavor or pursuing a personal goal that challenges you to step out of your comfort zone. Describe the goal you're pursuing and reflect on the mindset you intend to adopt throughout the journey. How will you embrace a growth mindset, viewing obstacles as opportunities for growth and setbacks as valuable learning experiences? Consider specific strategies you'll employ to maintain a positive and resilient mindset, even in the face of adversity. Then, visualize the potential impact of cultivating a growth mindset on your personal growth and achievement of the goal.

SMALL CHANGE 9:
COMMITTING TO GOALS

"Without goals and plans to reach them, you are like a ship that has set sail with no destination."

- FITZHUGH DODSON

Goal: A goal is like a picture of what you want in the future, something you plan and work hard to make happen.

Commit: When you commit to something, you're all in, fully dedicated to making it happen, like giving your all to reach your goal.

***

Imagine your dreams are stars in the night sky, and goals are the maps guiding you to reach them. In this chapter, we'll illuminate why setting goals is not merely a step but the very heartbeat of progress, bringing us nearer to the life we desire.

Just as embracing a growth mindset enriches our lives, setting and committing to meaningful goals aligned with our values can offer direction, purpose, and fulfillment. Within this segment, let's explore practical strategies for setting and committing to goals while overcoming obstacles and maintaining resilience along the way.

FINDING YOUR WAY WITH GOALS:

Goals are like destinations on a map, pointing you toward your dreams—those big things you want to achieve in life, like starting a business or retiring successfully. They serve as specific targets or objectives to aim for, guiding you along the path to what you desire.

But why are these destinations so important? Research shows that setting clear goals can boost your performance and keep you motivated, making life more fulfilling along the way.

Now, what do these goals actually look like? Consider the following shorter-term scenario: Your dream is to go on a trip, and the goal is to save enough money to pay for it. Each paycheck, you put away $50 toward your trip fund. These savings goals are like the checkpoints on your journey to your ultimate getaway. Each step you take, like the $50 of savings from every paycheck, brings you closer to your ultimate goal of jetting off on that adventure.

But it's not just about setting goals; it's also crucial to stick to them. So, how can we make sure that we remain on track, moving from one exciting destination to the next? Because staying committed to our goals is like discovering treasure at the end of the journey!

Let's start by looking at why it's important to stick to your goals and some straightforward strategies for setting them. Remember, it's not only about establishing goals; it's equally vital to adhere to them. We'll explore how maintaining commitment and completing each step on the path, even amidst challenges, can transform our aspirations into reality.

WHY STICKING TO YOUR GOALS MATTERS:

Maintaining resilience and staying committed to your goals involves more than just setting objectives; it requires dedication, perseverance, and a clear understanding of why those goals matter. According to Locke and Latham (2002), individuals who commit to their goals are more likely to achieve them and experience greater levels of life satisfaction. By aligning our goals with our values and aspirations, we create a roadmap for personal growth and fulfillment.

Setting meaningful goals that resonate with our values and aspirations is crucial for long-term commitment and motivation. Here are some examples of meaningful goals aligned with different areas of life:

Career: Striving for advancement in a field that reflects your passions and principles, such as aiming for a promotion in your current job or launching your own entrepreneurial venture.

Relationships: Forming deeper bonds with loved ones, setting goals to enhance communication by engaging in regular, meaningful conversations, dedicating weekly quality time with family or friends, or arranging a romantic retreat with your partner.

Health and Wellness: Establishing objectives for physical well-being, such as training to participate in a 5k race, attending yoga sessions three times weekly, or preparing nutritious lunches for work.

Personal Growth: Furthering aspirations for self-improvement, like pursuing new skills such as photography, learning to play a musical instrument, or committing to reading a new book monthly to broaden your knowledge and perspective.

So, whether it's advancing in your career, strengthening your relationships, improving your health, or growing personally, sticking to your goals is the key to enjoying a more fulfilling and satisfying life journey.

When you remain committed to your goals, you not only make progress toward your aspirations but also build confidence in your ability to overcome challenges. Each step forward reinforces your sense of purpose and brings you closer to the life you envision for yourself.

STRATEGIES FOR GOAL SETTING AND ACHIEVEMENT:

Effective goal setting involves a combination of clarity, specificity, and action planning. By breaking down larger goals into manageable steps and establishing a timeline for achievement, we create a straightforward roadmap for success. Additionally, employing strategies such as visualization, positive self-talk, and accountability can enhance motivation and momentum toward goal attainment.

Here are some practical strategies for goal setting and achievement:

SMART Goals: Set goals that are Specific, Measurable, Achievable, Relevant, and Time-bound.

Break it Down: Break larger goals into smaller, actionable steps to make them more manageable and achievable.

Create a Plan: Develop a detailed action plan outlining the steps needed to achieve each goal, including deadlines and milestones.

Visualize Success: Use visualization techniques to mentally rehearse achieving your goals and envision the outcomes you desire.

Stay Accountable: Share your goals with a supportive friend, family member, or mentor who can help keep you accountable and provide encouragement along the way.

Reaching our goals is like embarking on an epic quest—we need a clear map, small steps to guide us, and a cheerleading squad to keep us going. By setting SMART goals, breaking them down into bite-sized tasks, and visualizing success, we're arming ourselves with the tools we need for an exhilarating journey toward our dreams. So, let's suit up, grab our compass, and try out these strategies for an adventure-filled path to success!

THE BENEFITS OF ALIGNING GOALS WITH VALUES AND ASPIRATIONS:

Setting meaningful goals that resonate with our core values is more than just a strategy for achievement; it's the cornerstone of a fulfilling and purpose-driven life. When our goals are deeply connected to what we hold dear, they transcend mere targets and become powerful catalysts for personal growth and fulfillment. These goals not only reflect who we are but also ignite a profound sense of purpose and direction in our journey.

Aligning goals with our values lays a solid foundation for unwavering motivation and commitment. When our aspirations align with what truly matters to us, we are naturally inclined to persevere and remain resilient, even in the face of adversity. Our values serve as guiding stars, illuminating the path ahead and helping us navigate through life's challenges with clarity and determination.

Research underscores the importance of this alignment, showing that individuals who set goals consistent with their values experience a heightened sense of purpose, increased motivation, and overall greater happiness (Deci & Ryan, 2000).

Furthermore, studies published in the Journal of Positive Psychology have revealed that students who pursue goals aligned with their intrinsic values report higher levels of well-being and life satisfaction (Niemiec, Ryan, & Deci, 2009).

Before we charge ahead with our goals, let's make sure they match what's most important to us. It's like making sure our map is pointing in the right direction before we start our trip. When our goals match our values, it gives our journey a clear purpose and makes it more meaningful. So, let's start our journey with confidence, knowing that our aligned goals will lead us to success and happiness. And as we get going, let's figure out how to deal with challenges and stay motivated along the way.

OVERCOMING OBSTACLES AND STAYING MOTIVATED:

Despite our best efforts, obstacles and setbacks are inevitable on the journey toward goal achievement. However, resilience and perseverance are key to overcoming challenges and staying motivated. Whether it's a sudden change in circumstances, unexpected roadblocks, or moments of self-doubt, we all face hurdles along the way.

But with the right mindset and strategies in place, we can navigate through these challenges and emerge stronger than ever. Here are some strategies to tackle them:

Reframe Setbacks: Imagine you're working on a big project, and suddenly, you hit a roadblock. Instead of beating yourself up over it, see it as a chance to learn and grow. Maybe you realize a different approach could work better. This mindset shift is crucial when committing to goals, as it helps us stay resilient and focused, even in the face of challenges.

Seek Support: Picture yourself feeling overwhelmed with your goals. You reach out to a close friend or mentor for a pep talk, and they remind you of how far you've come and how capable you are. Their words give you the boost you need to keep going.

Celebrate Progress: Let's say you've been working on a personal goal for a while, like getting fit. Even if you've only managed to squeeze in a short workout today, take a moment to pat yourself on the back. Every little step forward counts, and recognizing your progress keeps you fired up.

Stay Flexible: You're on track to meet a deadline when suddenly, unexpected circumstances disrupt your plans. Instead of getting frustrated, you brainstorm alternative solutions and adjust your strategy accordingly. Being adaptable keeps you moving forward despite the setbacks.

Practice Self-Compassion: Imagine you're feeling discouraged because you didn't achieve as much as you hoped today. Instead of being hard on yourself, you take a moment to remind yourself that it's okay to have off days. Treating yourself with kindness helps you bounce back and tackle your goals with renewed energy.

Despite our best efforts, obstacles and setbacks are inevitable on the journey toward goal achievement. However, resilience and perseverance are key to overcoming challenges and staying motivated. Whether it's a sudden change in circumstances, unexpected roadblocks, or moments of self-doubt, we all face hurdles along the way.

But with the right mindset and strategies in place, we can navigate through these challenges and emerge stronger than ever. These strategies, like seeing setbacks as learning opportunities and celebrating your progress, can really help you keep your spirits up and your eyes on the prize! By embracing these approaches, not only do we overcome obstacles, but we also find greater fulfillment and success on our journey toward achieving our goals.

THE BENEFITS OF COMMITTING TO YOUR GOALS:

Committing to your goals brings numerous benefits. Just as aligning your goals with your values and aspirations is essential, committing to them enhances your productivity and overall well-being. Research by Locke and Latham (2002) underscores the significance of committing to specific and challenging goals for improved performance and motivation. Sharing your fitness achievements on social media increases your external accountability and motivates you to stick to your workout routines, improving your fitness levels and well-being. Goal pursuit provides you with a sense of purpose and direction in life, as highlighted by Sheldon and Elliot (1999).

Committing to learning new skills, like playing an instrument, leads to a sense of accomplishment and fulfillment, boosting your self-esteem and happiness. Achieving goals such as crossing the finish line of a marathon brings you pride and satisfaction, motivating you to set new goals and pursue further achievements. Committing to meaningful goals enriches your life beyond tangible outcomes, providing you with purpose, growth, and the opportunity to flourish.

So, when you commit to goals that truly matter to you, you're shaping your life in meaningful ways. By staying dedicated and pushing through challenges, you're not only boosting your productivity but also enhancing your overall well-being. Every step you take toward your goals brings you closer to the life you envision for yourself. And when you reach those milestones, whether big or small, it's not just about the achievement itself—it's about the sense of fulfillment and joy that comes with knowing you're moving in the right direction.

As you navigate the ups and downs of pursuing your goals, remember to stay focused, stay resilient, and, most importantly, stay true to what matters most to you. Because in the end, it's not just about reaching the finish line—it's about embracing the journey and becoming the best version of yourself along the way.

GOAL COMMITMENT THROUGH HABIT FORMATION:

Committing to goals is not just a one-time decision; it's an ongoing process that requires consistent effort and dedication. Habits are the actions we repeat regularly without conscious thought, and they play a crucial role in helping us stay committed to our goals. By incorporating goal-related habits and rituals into our daily lives, we reinforce our commitment and keep ourselves on track.

Whether it's setting aside dedicated time for goal-related tasks, visualizing success, or reflecting on progress, integrating these habits into our daily routines strengthens our resolve and momentum. These habits act as reminders of our aspirations and serve to align our actions with our long-term goals, making it easier to stay focused and motivated on our journey towards success.

Here are some strategies to help you commit to your goals through habit formation:

Set Aside Time: Schedule dedicated time each day or week to work on your goals and make progress toward achievement.

Visualize Success: Take a few minutes each day to visualize yourself achieving your goals and experiencing the outcomes you desire.

Reflect on Progress: Routinely review your progress toward your goals and celebrate your achievements, no matter how small.

Stay Consistent: Make goal-related tasks a regular part of your daily routine to maintain momentum and focus.

Stay Accountable: Frequently share your goals with someone who can help keep you accountable and provide support and encouragement.

These habits and rituals not only help us stick to our goals but also keep us feeling motivated and focused every day. By integrating them into our daily routines, we can strengthen our commitment and make steady progress toward achieving our aspirations.

PERSONAL STORIES ILLUSTRATING THE POWER OF WELL-SET GOALS AND COMMITMENT:

Next, experience the profound impact of well-set goals and unwavering commitment through two personal stories that illustrate how they can shape lives and bring dreams to fruition.

Aligning Goals with Values and Passions:

Aisha always had a passion for environmental conservation. She felt a deep connection to nature and wanted to make a positive impact on the planet. However, with a demanding job and busy schedule, it was easy for her to prioritize other responsibilities over her passion for environmental activism.

One day, Aisha attended a workshop on goal setting and learned about the importance of aligning goals with core values. Inspired by this idea, she set a goal to volunteer for a local environmental organization every weekend. This goal resonated deeply with her values and aspirations, providing her with a sense of purpose and direction in her life.

To ensure she didn't get overwhelmed, distracted, or stuck in the process, Aisha took proactive steps. She broke down her goal into smaller, manageable tasks, such as researching volunteer opportunities, contacting organizations, and scheduling her volunteering commitments in advance. By breaking her goal into actionable steps, Aisha was able to maintain focus and momentum without feeling overwhelmed by the magnitude of her commitment.

As Aisha immersed herself in volunteer work, she experienced a profound sense of fulfillment and satisfaction. She felt like she was making a meaningful contribution to a cause she cared about deeply. Over time, Aisha's commitment to her goal not only strengthened her connection to environmental activism but also enriched her life with purpose and meaning.

By staying organized, prioritizing her time effectively, and staying true to her values, Aisha was able to commit to her goals without getting overwhelmed or distracted. She remained focused on her purpose, allowing her passion for environmental conservation to drive her actions and shape her life in meaningful ways.

Understanding the Significance of Goal Commitment:

Mike dreamed of starting his own business but struggled to take the first step. He was afraid of failure and doubted his ability to succeed as an entrepreneur. Despite his fears, Mike knew that he would always regret not pursuing his dream if he didn't take action.

Determined to overcome his doubts and fears, Mike set a goal to launch his business within the next year. He committed to his goal by creating a detailed action plan, setting milestones, and seeking support from friends and mentors. Mike also reminded himself of the significance of his goal and the impact it would have on his life if he succeeded.

As Mike worked toward his goal, he encountered numerous challenges and setbacks. There were times when he felt overwhelmed and tempted to give up. However, Mike's commitment to his goal kept him focused and motivated. He reminded himself of the reasons why his goal was important to him and persisted in the face of adversity.

After months of hard work and dedication, Mike finally launched his business. Despite the challenges he faced along the way, Mike felt an immense sense of accomplishment and fulfillment. He realized that committing to his goal not only helped him achieve his dream but also taught him valuable lessons about resilience, perseverance, and the power of goal setting.

IN A NUTSHELL:

In this chapter, we've explored the life-changing power of setting and committing to meaningful goals. By aligning our goals with core values and aspirations and utilizing helpful habit creation, we've discovered how these simple changes can lead to significant impacts in various aspects of our lives, from career advancement to personal growth.

By reframing setbacks, seeking support, celebrating progress, and practicing self-compassion, we've equipped ourselves with the tools needed to navigate challenges with resilience and emerge stronger.

In the next chapter, we'll focus on pursuing personal growth. It's all about trying to get better at things and improving ourselves. This connects to what we talked about in this chapter on committing to our goals because sticking to our goals is a way to grow personally. So, by learning more about personal growth, we'll see how it helps us build on the commitment we've made to our goals and make our lives even better.

CONTINUING EDUCATION RESOURCES FOR COMMITTING TO GOALS:

1. *Goal Setting: How to Create an Action Plan and Achieve Your Goals* by Michael S. Dobson
2. *The Power of Habit: Why We Do What We Do in Life and Business* by Charles Duhigg

3. *Goals! How to Get Everything You Want Faster Than You Ever Thought Possible* by Brian Tracy

4. *The Achievement Habit: Stop Wishing, Start Doing, and Take Command of Your Life* by Bernard Roth

5. *Grit: The Power of Passion and Perseverance* by Angela Duckworth

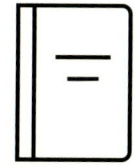

JOURNALING PROMPTS FOR COMMITTING TO GOALS:

Journaling prompts are a great way to help you engage with the material and reflect on your own experiences. Here are two prompts for this chapter:

Journal Prompt 1: Reflect on a time when you set a goal that was deeply aligned with your core values and aspirations. Describe the goal you set and the process of committing to it. How did aligning the goal with your values impact your motivation and determination to achieve it? Consider the challenges you encountered along the way and how your commitment to the goal helped you overcome them. Reflect on the sense of fulfillment and satisfaction you experienced upon achieving the goal and how it contributed to your overall well-being and sense of purpose.

Journal Prompt 2: Imagine yourself facing a significant obstacle or setback in the pursuit of a goal. How would you respond to this challenge, and what strategies would you employ to stay committed to your goal? Consider how reframing setbacks, seeking support, celebrating progress, staying flexible, and practicing self-compassion can help you maintain motivation and resilience. Reflect on the importance of perseverance and determination in overcoming obstacles and staying on course toward achieving your goals.

SMALL CHANGE 10:
PURSUING PERSONAL GROWTH

*"Growth is painful. Change is painful.
But nothing is as painful as staying stuck
somewhere you don't belong."*

- MANDY HALE

Personal growth: It's all about getting better at stuff like skills, knowledge, and habits, so you can be your best self and live your happiest, most successful life. It's like unlocking your full potential and becoming the person you want to be.

***

Starting a journey toward personal growth is like going on an exciting adventure within yourself. Every step you take opens up new chances to become the best version of you. After our discussion about sticking to goals, going after personal growth just naturally follows. It's like adding another layer to that commitment. Like when you set and work toward goals, focusing on personal growth keeps you growing and feeling fulfilled.

In this chapter, we'll talk about the role of personal growth in enhancing happiness, offer practical strategies for continuous learning and development, explain how to embrace challenges as opportunities for growth, and discuss the importance of setting intentions for personal growth and transformation.

We'll also draw upon our previous discussions on developing a growth mindset to highlight how personal growth involves not only acquiring new skills and knowledge but also pursuing a mindset that embraces challenges and views failures as opportunities for learning and improvement.

Current Research on the Benefits of Personal Growth:

Engaging in lifelong learning means exploring interests and hobbies that challenge you emotionally and intellectually. Research from the Harvard Business Review (Smith & Jones, 2023) suggests that this pursuit leads to higher levels of overall well-being and satisfaction. For example, learning a musical instrument or a new language not only stimulates your brain but also brings a sense of achievement and joy, reaping significant benefits.

Setting personal development goals is crucial for growth and provides numerous benefits. Studies published in the Journal of Applied Psychology (Brown et al., 2021) show that individuals who set specific, measurable goals for self-improvement are more likely to succeed and feel satisfied. Breaking down larger goals into smaller, actionable steps creates a roadmap for progress, leading to tangible benefits. For instance, improving time management skills by implementing a daily schedule can boost productivity and reduce stress, resulting in significant benefits for overall well-being.

Embracing feedback is vital for personal growth and yields considerable benefits. Research from Stanford University (Lee & Garcia, 2022) suggests that those who welcome feedback as a chance to grow tend to excel in both professional and personal life. Viewing feedback as constructive criticism helps identify areas for improvement, leading to numerous benefits. Actively seeking feedback, such as from colleagues on a work project, can lead to valuable insights and performance improvements, bringing about tangible benefits.

Stepping outside your comfort zone is key to expanding horizons and yields numerous benefits. Findings from the American Psychological Association (Johnson, 2020) indicate that regularly challenging yourself leads to higher levels of creativity and resilience. Whether it's traveling alone to a foreign country or speaking in public, stepping beyond familiar boundaries fosters personal growth and confidence, resulting in numerous benefits.

Engaging in lifelong learning, setting personal development goals, embracing feedback, and stepping outside your comfort zone are essential for personal growth and fulfillment. The research demonstrates that pursuing intellectual and emotional challenges not only develops curiosity and resilience but also leads to greater success and satisfaction in life, yielding numerous benefits.

ACTIONABLE STEPS FOR PERSONAL GROWTH AND CONTINUOUS LEARNING:

Personal growth and continuous learning go hand in hand, forming the cornerstone of a fulfilling life. These strategies not only help us adapt to change but also expand our horizons, seize new opportunities, and ultimately lead to greater happiness and satisfaction.

Here are some actionable steps to boost personal growth and support continuous learning:

Read Regularly: Make it a habit to cozy up with some good reads each day, whether it's articles, blogs, or the books you find at the end of our chapters in 'Continuing Education Resources.' They're like hidden gems waiting to sprinkle some knowledge magic into your life!

Attend Workshops or Seminars: Participate in events to gain new skills and knowledge.

Seek Mentorship: Connect with a mentor or coach for personalized guidance and unwavering support.

Reflect on Experiences: Set aside time to reflect deeply on your experiences, extracting valuable lessons for ongoing personal growth and development.

Engage in Lifelong Learning: Pursue interests and hobbies that challenge you intellectually and emotionally.

Set personal Development Goals: Identify areas for improvement and create actionable steps to achieve them.

Embrace Feedback: View feedback as constructive criticism to enhance skills and create better outcomes.

Step Outside Your Comfort Zone: Take calculated risks and explore new experiences to expand your horizons.

By doing things like reading, going to workshops, finding mentors, and thinking about our experiences, we're growing. Each step brings us closer to our best selves. So, let's dive into personal growth with excitement. Let's keep learning, setting development goals, listening to feedback, and trying new things. These actions make life better and help us make our dreams come true.

SETTING INTENTIONS FOR PERSONAL GROWTH AND DEVELOPMENT:

Setting intentions for personal growth involves more than just wishful thinking; it's about intentionally aligning your actions with your values and aspirations. By clarifying what truly matters to you and actively working toward those goals, you can pave the way for meaningful growth and development in your life.

Here are some practical ways to set intentions for personal growth:

Define your Values: Take some time to reflect on what truly matters to you. Identify your core values – the principles that guide your life and decisions. Then, align your goals with these values. For example, if family is a core value, setting intentions to spend quality time with loved ones can be a meaningful goal.

Visualize Success: Picture yourself achieving your goals and embodying the person you aspire to be. Visualization is a powerful tool that can help you stay motivated and focused on your journey of personal growth. Close your eyes and imagine yourself succeeding, feeling the emotions of accomplishment and fulfillment.

Create a Vision Board: Compile images, quotes, and affirmations that represent your goals and aspirations. Creating a visual representation of your intentions can serve as a daily reminder of what you're working toward. Place your vision board somewhere you'll see it often, like your bedroom or workspace, to keep your goals top of mind.

Develop a Growth Mindset: Elevate your belief in your ability to learn, grow, and adapt in the face of challenges. Embrace setbacks as opportunities for growth rather than roadblocks. Cultivate a mindset of curiosity and resilience, and remember that personal growth is a journey, not a destination.

Setting intentions for personal growth is a powerful way to take control of your life and create the future you desire. By aligning your actions with your values and aspirations, you can cultivate a life that is meaningful, fulfilling, and true to who you are. Remember, personal growth is a journey that requires dedication, perseverance, and self-reflection. Embrace the process, stay committed to your intentions, and watch as you blossom into the best version of yourself.

Managing Life's Challenges to Learn and Grow:

Life often throws unexpected challenges our way, doesn't it? But here's the thing: those bumps in the road aren't dead ends; they're chances for us to grow and become better.

Imagine this: you're going about your day smoothly, and suddenly, you hit a roadblock. Maybe it's a big project at work that seems overwhelming, a disagreement with a close friend, or just feeling stuck in a rut. Instead of feeling defeated, you decide to tackle it head-on, knowing that every obstacle presents an opportunity to learn and improve.

Now, let's roll up our sleeves and get to work. Dealing with challenges as chances for personal growth is more than just putting on a brave face. It means taking action. Consider asking for advice from someone you trust, like a mentor or a friend, to get some helpful tips. Picture breaking down big goals into smaller, manageable steps, like you'd break levels in a video game. And don't forget to be kind to yourself along the way—it's important for staying strong.

By seeing challenges as opportunities to become better, you're not just overcoming them—you're growing from them. Think of it like a muscle that gets stronger with each workout. With this in mind, you'll handle life's ups and downs with confidence and determination, knowing that every challenge brings you one step closer to your full potential. And that's how you release your full potential and find lasting happiness.

PERSONAL STORIES OF PERSONAL GROWTH AND DEVELOPMENT:

Prepare to be inspired by these two firsthand accounts of personal growth and development journeys:

The Journey of Personal Growth Through Self-Discovery:

Sophie always felt like something was missing in her life. Despite having friends and hobbies, she sensed there was more to discover about herself. She wanted to grow personally and find deeper meaning by making a positive impact on others' lives.

Determined to embark on a journey of self-discovery, Sophie began exploring ways to help people achieve their goals and dreams. She volunteered at a local community center, offering her time and skills to support those in need. Whether it was tutoring students, mentoring aspiring entrepreneurs, or simply lending a listening ear, Sophie found joy in helping others succeed.

During this voyage of personal growth, Sophie discovered her passion for coaching and mentorship.

Guiding others on their journeys filled her with a sense of purpose and fulfillment she had never experienced before. It was a revelation that ignited a fire within her to make a difference in the lives of those around her.

With this newfound passion guiding her personal growth, Sophie made intentional efforts to expand her impact. She enrolled in coaching courses, honed her skills, and sought opportunities to connect with more people who could benefit from her guidance and support.

In the end, Sophie's journey of personal growth and self-discovery wasn't just about finding a new passion—it was about making a meaningful difference in the world. It had its challenges and moments of doubt, but also moments of profound joy and fulfillment. Through her journey, Sophie realized that by helping others achieve their dreams, she was also fulfilling her own.

The Power of Intention:

Jake had always been someone with big dreams and a drive to succeed. He was always pushing himself to reach his goals and move up the career ladder. But despite all his achievements, he couldn't shake the feeling that something was missing – a feeling of contentment and fulfillment in his life.

Inspired by the idea of personal growth, Jake decided to take a different approach. He started setting intentions for his own development and growth. It wasn't easy at first. There were times when he felt lost and unsure of what he really wanted. But he kept at it, determined to find clarity and fulfillment.

To help him on his journey, Jake began practicing mindfulness and self-reflection. Every day, he set aside time to think about his goals and what he wanted to achieve. It was a process of digging deep into himself, figuring out what truly mattered to him and what he wanted his life to look like.

As Jake embraced the idea of forging ahead with deliberate intent, he found fulfillment in the simple things, like spending quality time with loved ones, pursuing hobbies that brought him joy, and making a positive impact in his community. It was these moments of connection and contribution that brought him the most happiness and satisfaction.

Through this intentional approach to personal growth, Jake began to see things more clearly. He discovered a newfound sense of certainty and direction, aligning his actions with his values and aspirations. It was like a weight had been lifted off his shoulders, and he finally felt like he was on the right path.

IN A NUTSHELL:

Pursuing personal growth is an ongoing journey that involves continuous learning, self-reflection, and intentional development. By employing strategies such as setting personal development goals, embracing feedback, and courageously overcoming obstacles on your path to growth, you can ignite your own journey of personal growth and development. These strategies will not only help you increase your self-awareness and reach your full potential but also enable you to live with purpose and meaning.

In the next chapter, we'll explore the important topic of building resilience and its significant impact on personal and professional development. Understanding the principles of resilience and applying them to various areas of life can strengthen your ability to overcome challenges, adapt, and seize new opportunities for growth and success, empowering you to never give up on living your dream.

CONTINUING EDUCATION RESOURCES FOR PURSUING PERSONAL GROWTH:

1. *The Obstacle Is the Way: The Timeless Art of Turning Trials into Triumph* by Ryan Holiday
2. *You Are a Badass: How to Stop Doubting Your Greatness and Start Living an Awesome Life* by Jen Sincero
3. *The Subtle Art of Not Giving a F*ck: A Counterintuitive Approach to Living a Good Life* by Mark Manson
4. *Big Magic: Creative Living Beyond Fear* by Elizabeth Gilbert
5. *The Miracle Morning: The Not-So-Obvious Secret Guaranteed to Transform Your Life (Before 8AM)* by Hal Elrod

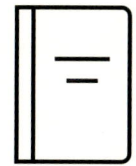

JOURNALING PROMPTS FOR PURSUING PERSONAL GROWTH:

Journaling prompts are a great way to help you engage with the material and reflect on your own experiences. Here are two prompts for this chapter:

Journal Prompt 1: Reflect on a time when you embarked on a journey of personal growth and development. Describe the challenges you faced along the way and how you approached them as opportunities for growth. Consider the strategies you employed to overcome obstacles, such as setting intentions, seeking feedback, and stepping outside your comfort zone. Reflect on how this journey impacted your self-awareness, resilience, and overall well-being and how it contributed to your personal growth and fulfillment.

Journal Prompt 2: Imagine yourself setting intentions for personal growth and transformation in various areas of your life, such as career, relationships, health, or personal development. Describe specific goals or aspirations you would like to achieve in each of these areas and how you would align your actions with your intentions. Consider the strategies you would use to foster continuous learning and development, embrace challenges as opportunities for growth, and cultivate a growth mindset. Reflect on how setting these intentions can enhance your sense of purpose, fulfillment, and overall well-being as you pursue your journey of personal growth.

SMALL CHANGE 11: BUILDING RESILIENCE

"Resilience is not what happens to you. It's how you react to, respond to, and recover from what happens to you."

-   JEFFREY GITOMER

Resilience: Think of it as your bounce-back power when life gets tough. It's all about handling challenges, staying confident, and leaning on friends and family for support.

***

How do we bounce back when life knocks us down? When things get tough, our resilience is what helps us not only survive but also thrive. This chapter explores why resilience is crucial in overcoming life's challenges, offering practical insights, strategies, and real-life examples to empower you to understand and build resilience. By recognizing how even small changes in our resilience can lead to big impacts in improving our lives, you can navigate life's ups and downs effectively.

Resilience is like our inner springboard, the bounce-back ability we have to adapt and grow stronger when faced with adversity. It's not about avoiding difficulties altogether but rather about how we respond to them. Resilience encompasses qualities like perseverance, flexibility, and optimism, allowing us to weather life's storms with grace and resilience, allowing us to bounce back from setbacks, learn from experiences, and emerge even stronger than before.

RESEARCH ON USING RESILIENCE TO HANDLE ADVERSITY:

Studies indicate that resilient individuals tend to enjoy greater life satisfaction, psychological well-being, and overall success (Smith & Johnson, 2019). They cope better with stress, overcome obstacles, and maintain a positive outlook, even in tough circumstances.

For instance, let's look at the journey of Barbara, a single parent who faced the challenge of losing her job during a downturn in the business cycle. Despite the financial uncertainty and the added pressures of single parenthood, Barbara exemplified resilience. Instead of letting setbacks define her, she viewed the situation as an opportunity for growth. Barbara reached out to her support network for guidance, actively pursued new job opportunities, and dedicated herself to honing her skills.

Through perseverance and determination, Barbara not only secured a new job but also discovered a renewed sense of purpose and resilience that guided her through the toughest times.

Leading experts like Dr. Angela Duckworth and Dr. Martin Seligman highlight resilience as a key predictor of achievement and well-being. Duckworth defines it as perseverance and passion for long-term goals despite adversity, while Seligman emphasizes techniques like cognitive restructuring and fostering a positive outlook.

Resilient individuals experience lower levels of stress, anxiety, and depression, along with higher life satisfaction and optimism (Smith & Johnson, 2019). This is backed by research from sources like the American Psychological Association and the Journal of Applied Psychology, stressing resilience's positive impact on mental health and overall quality of life.

In conclusion, resilience is not just about bouncing back; it's about thriving in the face of adversity. By building resilience, we equip ourselves to tackle life's challenges with determination and emerge stronger, fostering lasting fulfillment.

BUILDING EMOTIONAL RESILIENCE THROUGH COPING STRATEGIES:

Think of emotional resilience as a kind of inner strength that helps you handle tough feelings like stress, letdowns, or sadness, and then bounce back stronger. It's about expanding our existing toolkit of healthy ways to deal with those emotions so they don't overwhelm you.

Imagine you're going through a rough patch in your personal life, maybe a tough breakup. Instead of letting it consume you, you turn to your coping strategies toolkit. You might lean on friends or family for support, journal your thoughts and feelings, or spend time doing activities that bring you joy, like hiking or painting.

These strategies help you weather the storm of emotions, gradually finding your footing and moving forward, even when it feels like the world's turned upside down.

Now, let's explore a few important coping strategies to learn and practice for building emotional resilience:

Practice Mindfulness: Mindfulness techniques, such as meditation and deep breathing exercises, can help you stay present and calm in the face of challenges, reducing stress and promoting emotional resilience.

Engage in Self-Care Activities: Taking care of your physical, mental, and emotional well-being through activities like exercise, adequate sleep, and hobbies you enjoy can replenish your energy and strengthen your ability to cope with adversity.

Seek Social Support: Connecting with friends, family, or a support network can provide a sense of belonging and validation, offering emotional support and perspective during difficult times. Sharing your thoughts and feelings with trusted individuals can alleviate stress and foster resilience.

Develop Problem-Solving Skills: Learning how to effectively address challenges and find solutions can build confidence and resilience. By breaking down problems into manageable steps and taking proactive actions, you can feel more empowered and resilient in the face of adversity.

Cultivate Optimism: Maintaining a positive outlook and focusing on hopeful possibilities, even in challenging situations, can enhance emotional resilience. By reframing negative thoughts and beliefs, you can cultivate resilience and adaptability, enabling you to bounce back from setbacks with resilience and determination.

Imagine you and your partner facing the heartbreak of a miscarriage after months of hoping to start a family. In the aftermath of your loss, you find solace in each other's support and seek counseling to process your grief together. Through open communication, mutual understanding, and shared coping strategies, you navigate your emotional journey with resilience, emerging stronger and more connected than before.

BUILDING INNER STRENGTH THROUGH MENTAL TOUGHNESS:

Think of mental toughness as your inner coach, cheering you on even when the going gets tough. It's all about staying focused, determined, and resilient, no matter what life throws your way. Just like with emotional resilience, building mental toughness means you're able to keep pushing forward, even when things seem impossible.

Imagine pouring your heart into renovating an old house, facing setbacks and stress along the way. Despite the challenges, you remain steadfast in your determination. You embrace risks and discomfort as part of the journey, using setbacks as fuel to drive you forward toward your goals of creating a cozy home for your family.

Now, picture yourself facing a difficult family situation, encountering obstacles and doubts along the way. Despite the challenges, you tap into your inner strength. With a positive mindset and determination, you tackle each hurdle head-on. Though it's not easy, your resilience not only pushes you through but also leaves you stronger and more capable.

So, whether it's at work, in relationships, or facing personal challenges, strengthening your mental toughness is like building a muscle—you've got to work at it every day. It's about staying disciplined, talking yourself up, and embracing discomfort as a chance to learn and grow.

PRACTICAL EXERCISES AND ACTIVITIES TO BUILD RESILIENCE:

Building resilience is like taking your inner strength to the next level. It's about more than just coping with tough times—it's about actively training yourself to bounce back stronger than before.

These strategies go beyond the coping strategies we talked about earlier. While coping strategies help you manage emotions in the moment, building resilience involves specific exercises and activities that strengthen your ability to bounce back from adversity over the long haul.

Here are some practical strategies to help you develop resilience in your daily life:

Gratitude Journaling: Take a few minutes each day to write down things you're grateful for. Focusing on positive aspects of your life can shift your perspective and build resilience.

Positive Affirmations: Repeat positive affirmations to yourself regularly, such as "I am strong," "I am capable," and "I can overcome challenges." These affirmations can help reinforce a positive mindset and boost resilience.

Visualization Techniques: Imagine yourself successfully overcoming challenges and achieving your goals. Visualizing positive outcomes can increase confidence and resilience in difficult situations.

Goal Setting: Set realistic, achievable goals for yourself and work toward them gradually. Achieving small victories can boost confidence and resilience over time.

Physical Exercise: Engage in regular physical activity to reduce stress and improve mental resilience. Exercise releases endorphins, which can enhance mood and resilience.

Mindfulness Meditation: Practice mindfulness meditation to cultivate awareness of your thoughts and emotions. Mindfulness can help you stay calm and centered during challenging times, enhancing resilience.

Social Connections: Build strong relationships with friends, family, and community members. Social support is a key factor in resilience, providing emotional support and encouragement during difficult times.

Building resilience is like leveling up your inner strength to ninja status. It's about training yourself to bounce back stronger, like a seasoned warrior facing adversity head-on. These strategies are your secret weapons, honing your ability to overcome life's obstacles with finesse and determination.

With practice, you'll become a master of resilience, ready to tackle any challenge with confidence and grace. Incorporate these savvy practices into your daily routine, and watch your resilience reach legendary levels!

PERSONAL STORIES OF RESILIENCE:

Here are two inspiring stories of resilience, where individuals faced tough times head-on and came out stronger than ever:

Overcoming Setbacks Through Perseverance:

David had always dreamed of pursuing a career in music, particularly in the realm of blues. Inspired by legends like B.B. King, he poured his heart and soul into honing his craft, spending countless hours practicing his guitar and perfecting his vocals. However, just as he was on the brink of breaking into the industry, he faced a series of setbacks that threatened to derail his dreams.

First, David's bandmates decided to pursue other opportunities, leaving him to navigate the music scene alone. Then, a string of rejections from record labels and talent scouts left him feeling discouraged and defeated. To make matters worse, financial struggles forced him to take on odd jobs to make ends meet, leaving him with little time or energy to focus on his music.

Despite the challenges stacked against him, David refused to give up. He continued to write songs and perform at local venues, determined to prove his worth as a blues musician. He sought guidance from mentors in the industry, soaking up their advice and learning from their experiences. He embraced every opportunity to showcase his talent, from open mic nights to local festivals, seizing each chance to share his music with the world.

Months turned into years, but David's perseverance never wavered. He poured his heart and soul into his music, pouring his pain and struggles into his lyrics. Slowly but surely, his hard work began to pay off. He caught the attention of a small independent record label, who saw the potential in his unique sound and raw talent.

With their support, David released his debut album to critical acclaim, earning praise for his heartfelt lyrics and soulful melodies. His music resonated with listeners around the world, touching hearts and inspiring hope in the face of adversity. Through his journey of resilience, David proved that with passion, perseverance, and a belief in oneself, anything is possible.

Rising Above Adversity in the Workplace:

Sarah had always dreamed of climbing the corporate ladder. She worked tirelessly, dedicating all her energy and passion to her career. However, just as she was on the brink of a promotion, she was blindsided by a sudden downturn in the economy. The company she worked for downsized, and Sarah found herself facing a layoff.

At first, Sarah was devastated. She felt like she had lost everything she had worked so hard for. But deep down, she knew she couldn't let this setback define her. With determination and resilience, Sarah picked herself up and started exploring new opportunities.

She reached out to her professional network, seeking advice and job leads. She took courses to expand her skill set and improve her marketability. She embraced the uncertainty of her situation, viewing it as a chance to reinvent herself and pursue her passions.

Months passed, and Sarah's perseverance paid off. She landed a new job at a smaller company, where her talents were valued and her contributions recognized. Through the challenges she faced, Sarah emerged stronger and more resilient than ever before. She learned that setbacks are not the end of the road but rather opportunities for growth and self-discovery. In the face of adversity, Sarah found the courage to rise above and thrive.

In a Nutshell:

In your journey toward a better life, resilience is your loyal friend. It's what helps you handle tough times and come out stronger. By getting better at dealing with your emotions, toughening up mentally, and finding ways to cope, you're not just getting back up after a fall—you're getting stronger each time.

Whether you're dealing with personal problems, work challenges, or just life's ups and downs, resilience is like having a reliable anchor. So, lean on it like a trusted friend, tapping into your inner strength. Remember, you're stronger than you think.

And don't forget the practical exercises and activities we discussed to build resilience—those small, everyday actions that help you grow stronger. With resilience on your side, you're not just getting through; you're thriving, making your life better, and feeling more fulfilled along the way.

I've mentioned this before, but as we wrap up our discussion on building resilience, you might notice that these methods share similarities with the strategies we've explored for making significant changes in other aspects of your life. This isn't a coincidence. Mastering these skills in your toolkit not only strengthens your ability to bounce back from adversity but also equips you to tackle a wide range of challenges with greater effectiveness.

CONTINUING EDUCATION RESOURCES FOR BUILDING RESILIENCE:

1. *The Resilience Factor: 7 Keys to Finding Your Inner Strength and Overcoming Life's Hurdles* by Karen Reivich and Andrew Shatte
2. *Option B: Facing Adversity, Building Resilience, and Finding Joy* by Sheryl Sandberg and Adam Grant
3. *The Resilience Breakthrough: 27 Tools for Turning Adversity into Action* by Christian Moore
4. *Resilient: How to Grow an Unshakable Core of Calm, Strength, and Happiness* by Rick Hanson
5. *The Road to Resilience: From Chaos to Celebration* by Larry Dill and Terry Fralich

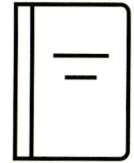

JOURNALING PROMPTS FOR BUILDING RESILIENCE:

Journaling prompts are a great way to help you engage with the material and reflect on your own experiences. Here are two prompts for this chapter:

Journal Prompt 1: Recall a time when you faced a significant challenge or setback in your life. Reflect on how you initially responded to the situation and the emotions you experienced. Consider the coping strategies you employed to navigate through the difficulty. Did you seek support from others, engage in self-care activities, or practice mindfulness techniques? Describe how these strategies helped you build resilience and bounce back from the adversity. Reflect on what you learned about yourself and your capacity for resilience through this experience.

Journal Prompt 2: Imagine yourself facing a daunting challenge or unexpected change in your life right now. How would you approach the situation with resilience? Consider the practical strategies and exercises discussed in the chapter, such as gratitude journaling, positive affirmations, visualization techniques, and social connections. Describe how you would apply these strategies to strengthen your resilience and navigate through the challenge effectively. Reflect on the potential growth and learning opportunities that could arise from embracing resilience in the face of adversity.

SMALL CHANGE 12: HARNESSING VISUALIZATION

"Visualization is daydreaming with a purpose."

- ROBERT FOSTER BENNETT

Visualization: Picture it as crafting a movie in your mind, where you envision various scenarios or scenes without relying on your eyes.

***

Close your eyes and picture this: you're standing on a beach, feeling the warm sand beneath your feet, and hearing the gentle crash of waves. Now imagine you're visualizing your dream vacation—every detail from the vibrant colors of the sunset to the taste of the exotic cuisine. This is just a glimpse of the power of visualization.

Like resilience, which helps us bounce back from tough times, visualization lets us craft our future before it even happens. It's like being the director of your own movie, where you get to script the scenes of success and triumph.

When we tap into visualization, we're essentially giving ourselves a remarkable skill—an ability to adapt to challenges and conquer obstacles. By picturing ourselves achieving our goals, we're priming our minds for success, building a resilient mindset that can weather any storm.

In this chapter, we're diving into the world of visualization techniques. We'll uncover how these practices can supercharge our journey of rising and thriving, helping us elevate our lives to new heights we once only dreamed of reaching. So, get ready to unleash the power of your imagination and discover how visualization can improve your life.

RESEARCH ON THE BENEFITS OF VISUALIZATION:

Visualization, also known as mental imagery, involves creating vivid mental images or scenarios to enhance performance in various domains, such as sports, academics, and personal development. Beyond its primary application, visualization offers a multitude of benefits for overall well-being and goal attainment.

One significant advantage of visualization is its ability to reduce stress and anxiety. By immersing oneself in mental landscapes where challenges are overcome and goals are achieved, individuals can experience a sense of calm and confidence. Research by Dr. Sarah Lazar (2000) indicates that regular visualization practice can lead to reductions in stress levels and increased feelings of relaxation and tranquility.

Moreover, visualization serves as a powerful motivator, igniting the drive and determination needed to pursue aspirations. By vividly envisioning desired outcomes, individuals can fuel a sense of purpose and direction, propelling them forward on their journey to success. Dr.

Carol Dweck (2006) emphasizes visualization's role in developing a growth mindset, where challenges are perceived as opportunities for growth and progress.

In addition to its psychological benefits, visualization can impact physical health and well-being. Studies by Dr. Herbert Benson (1975) demonstrate that visualization techniques, combined with relaxation exercises, can improve cardiovascular health and immune function. By harnessing visualization, individuals can tap into their body's innate healing mechanisms, promoting overall health and vitality.

Research also consistently highlights the powerful impact of visualization on our lives, shaping our thoughts, emotions, and actions toward desired outcomes. For instance, a study by Kappes et al. (2012) found that visualization enhances cognitive processes related to goal setting and achievement.

Imagine someone envisioning themselves performing exceptionally well in a job interview, rehearsing each step in their mind before the big day. This mental preparation can significantly boost their confidence and performance.

Athletes who incorporate visualization techniques into their training routines often experience significant performance improvements. Studies published in the Journal of Applied Sport Psychology (Vealey et al., 1992) have shown that visualizing successful athletic performances can lead to better actual performance outcomes.

Picture a basketball player mentally rehearsing every shot and play before a game. This mental imagery can sharpen their skills and boost their game-day performance.

Dr. Ellen Langer (2009) highlights how visualization influences both mindset and physiological responses, preparing our minds and bodies for success.

For example, imagine someone visualizing themselves delivering a confident presentation at work. This mental rehearsal can help reduce anxiety and increase their chances of delivering a successful presentation.

In essence, visualization empowers us to live our best lives by clarifying goals, increasing motivation, and overcoming challenges with greater ease. By integrating visualization into our daily routines, we open up new pathways to success and fulfillment, ultimately transforming our lives for the better.

TIPS TO INCORPORATE VISUALIZATION INTO YOUR DAILY LIFE:

Visualization is a powerful technique that uses your imagination to help calm your mind and reduce stress. By picturing peaceful or positive scenes in your head, you can create feelings of calmness and clarity, which can help counteract stress and anxiety. Incorporating visualization into your daily routine is not just about sporadically imagining your goals; it's about making it a consistent practice that deeply impacts your mindset and actions.

By setting aside dedicated time for visualization exercises, you create a ritual that reinforces your goals and strengthens your commitment to achieving them. Just like any skill or habit, the more you practice visualization, the more powerful it becomes in shaping your reality.

Let's explore some practical tips on how you can integrate visualization into your daily routine to reap its benefits:

Create a Visualization Journal: Start by writing down specific scenarios or goals you want to imagine in your mind. Describe these scenes in detail, including sights, sounds, and feelings.

Practice Relaxation Techniques: Before you begin visualizing, take a few deep breaths to relax your body and mind. This can help you get into a more focused and receptive state for visualization.

Use Guided Imagery: Find guided visualization recordings or videos online that lead you through relaxing scenes or scenarios. These can be helpful if you're new to visualization or if you prefer a more structured approach.

Engage Your Senses: As you visualize, try to incorporate all your senses. Imagine the sights, sounds, smells, tastes, and textures of the scene you're picturing to make it feel more real and immersive.

Be Patient and Persistent: Like any skill, visualization takes practice. Don't get discouraged if it feels challenging at first. Keep practicing regularly, and over time, you'll likely find it easier and more effective.

Let's imagine you practicing visualization during your morning routine. Instead of just going through the motions, use these tips to turn it into a mini visualization session. As you brush your teeth or get dressed, start picturing yourself achieving your goals—a successful presentation at work, a fun day with friends, or a healthy lifestyle. With each mental image, fully engage, leaving no room for negative thoughts. Instead of feeling anxious, feel inspired and confident.

Now, think about a different situation. Picture yourself stuck in traffic on your way to work. Instead of getting frustrated, close your eyes and start to visualize your ideal commute—smooth traffic, green lights all the way, and arriving at work feeling calm and focused. By visualizing positive outcomes, let go of tension and find peace amidst the chaos of the commute.

Incorporating visualization into your daily routine is key to maximizing its effectiveness. By setting aside dedicated time for visualization exercises, you can cultivate a regular practice that reinforces your goals and strengthens your commitment to achieving them.

Whether it's through guided visualization sessions, journaling, or creating vision boards, finding a visualization technique that resonates with you is rewarding. By integrating visualization into your daily routine, you can harness its influential potential to reflect your aspirations and create the life you desire.

PRACTICAL STRATEGIES FOR EFFECTIVE VISUALIZATION:

By regularly engaging in visualization, you train your mind to recognize opportunities and stay focused on your objectives. These strategies build on the tips we just covered, reinforcing the power of visualization to enhance your resilience and commitment.

Here are some practical strategies that can supercharge your visualization game and turbocharge your path to success:

Define Goals Clearly: Start by getting crystal clear about what you want to achieve. Define your goals and objectives with laser precision.

Create Dedicated Space: Find a quiet spot where you can focus without interruptions. Set aside dedicated time for your visualization practice, whether it's first thing in the morning or before you retire at night.

Visualize with All Senses: When you visualize, don't hold back—make it as vivid and real as possible. Engage all your senses. Feel the warmth of the sun on your skin, hear the sound of applause, smell the scent of success. The more detailed, the better.

Use Positive Affirmations: Boost your visualization power with affirmations and positive self-talk. Remind yourself of your strengths, your capabilities, and your worthiness of success.

Track Progress and Celebrate: Keep track of your progress. Regularly check in with yourself to see how far you've come. Celebrate your wins, no matter how small, and use them to fuel your motivation to keep pushing forward.

By weaving these practical strategies into your visualization routine, you're not just daydreaming—you're laying the groundwork for real, tangible success. So, grab your mental paintbrush, start picturing your dreams, and get ready to turn them into reality.

CREATING VIVID MENTAL IMAGERY TO ENHANCE PERFORMANCE:

We've already explored how powerful visualization can be for setting and achieving your goals. But did you know it can also be a game-changer for improving performance in various areas of your life? Whether you're an athlete, performer, or professional, visualizing success can help you nail your game.

When we conjure up super-clear mental pictures of what we want to achieve, it's like turbocharging our confidence, focus, and performance. Picture this: You're gearing up for a big presentation. Instead of sweating bullets, you close your eyes and picture yourself acing every slide, nailing every point, and leaving your audience in awe. By painting this vivid mental picture, you're getting yourself pumped and primed for success.

Take a pro athlete, for example. They might close their eyes and imagine themselves zooming across the finish line, leaving their rivals in the dust. They feel the rush of victory, hear the roar of the crowd, and soak up every moment of glory. By playing out this scene in their mind, they're boosting their confidence and getting mentally prepped for the big race.

Or think about a musician gearing up for a concert. They might visualize themselves flawlessly playing every note, with the crowd going wild for an encore. By rehearsing this mental concert in their mind, they're gearing up to deliver a performance that'll blow everyone away.

These examples show how vivid mental imagery through visualization can seriously level up your performance, whether you're on the field, on the stage, or in the boardroom. So next time you're gearing up for a big moment, close your eyes, picture success, and get ready to crush it.

PERSONAL STORIES ABOUT THE IMPACT OF VISUALIZATION ON SUCCESS:

Next, let's explore two personal stories that showcase the impact of visualization, underscoring its capacity to shape lives and open doors for progress and achievement.

Maya's Journey to Success:

Maya had always dreamed of starting her own business but felt overwhelmed by the challenges ahead. She struggled with self-doubt and uncertainty about whether she could turn her dream into reality.

However, Maya decided to incorporate visualization into her daily routine. Each morning, she carved out dedicated time to sit quietly and visualize herself running a successful business. She imagined every detail, from the layout of her office to the interactions with clients and the achievement of her financial goals. Maya immersed herself in this mental imagery, letting herself feel the excitement and satisfaction of accomplishing her dreams.

Through this practice, Maya gradually began to feel more confident and focused on her vision. She found herself inspired to take action, fueled by the vivid images of success she conjured in her mind.

As Maya continued to visualize her goals, she noticed a shift in her mindset. She became more proactive in pursuing her business idea, taking concrete steps like drafting a business plan, setting up meetings with potential clients, and attending networking events within her industry. Maya pushed through setbacks and challenges with determination, holding onto the belief that her vision was achievable.

Despite facing obstacles along the way, Maya remained resilient and unwavering in her pursuit of success. Her dedication and perseverance eventually paid off, and she successfully launched her business, turning her dream into a thriving reality.

Through the power of visualization, Maya not only overcame obstacles but also stayed motivated and achieved her entrepreneurial goals. The mental imagery she cultivated became a guiding force, helping her navigate challenges and stay focused on her path to success.

Liam's Journey to Personal Growth:

Liam had always struggled with public speaking, often feeling anxious and insecure when presenting in front of others. Despite his fear, Liam recognized that improving his communication skills was crucial for his career advancement.

Determined to conquer his fear, Liam decided to incorporate visualization techniques into his preparation process before each presentation. He would find a quiet space, close his eyes, and visualize himself speaking confidently on stage. Liam imagined himself engaging the audience with his words, exuding charisma, and delivering his message with clarity and conviction.

Through consistent visualization practice, Liam began to notice a significant improvement in his public speaking abilities. As he visualized himself succeeding in his mind's eye, he started to believe in his capabilities more strongly. With each mental rehearsal, Liam felt his confidence grow, and his nerves gradually began to subside.

When it came time to deliver his presentations, Liam felt more composed and assured than ever before. He no longer dreaded public speaking but instead saw it as an opportunity to showcase his skills and expertise. Liam's newfound confidence was evident to his colleagues, who noticed a marked improvement in his delivery style and stage presence.

By harnessing the power of visualization, Liam transformed his fear of public speaking into a strength. Through diligent practice and unwavering determination, he achieved personal growth and professional success. The visualization techniques he adopted became an integral part of his preparation routine, enabling him to overcome obstacles and excel in his career.

In a Nutshell:

Visualization is a potent tool for goal achievement, performance enhancement, and personal growth. By harnessing the power of our imagination, you can clarify your goals, increase motivation, and manifest your aspirations into reality. As you continue to integrate visualization into your daily routine, you empower yourself to embrace resilience, overcome challenges, and thrive in all aspects of your life.

Incorporating visualization into your routine not only helps you stay focused and motivated but also strengthens your belief in your ability to succeed, ultimately leading to greater fulfillment and success.

In the next chapter, we'll explore the importance of learning confidence and how it enhances our journey of personal growth and achievement, building upon the foundation of visualization to further empower ourselves in realizing our dreams.

Continuing Education Resources for Harnessing Visualization:

1. *Creative Visualization: Use the Power of Your Imagination to Create What You Want in Your Life* by Shakti Gawain
2. *The Visualization Toolkit: A Practical Guide to Visualizing for Success* by David G. Smith

3. *Visualization for Change: A Step-by-Step Guide to Creating Your Life from the Inside Out* by Lisa Nichols

4. *Visualize Your Way to Success: How to Harness the Power of Visualization to Achieve Your Personal and Professional Goals* by David L. Roger

5. *The Power of Visualization: Mindfulness Meditation for Corporate Change* by Martin L Ross

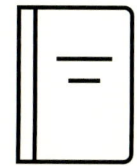

JOURNALING PROMPTS FOR HARNESSING VISUALIZATION:

Journaling prompts are a great way to help you engage with the material and reflect on your own experiences. Here are two prompts for this chapter:

Journal Prompt 1: Close your eyes and take a few deep breaths. Visualize yourself achieving one of your biggest goals or dreams. Picture every detail vividly, from the sights and sounds to the emotions you experience. As you immerse yourself in this mental imagery, reflect on how it makes you feel. How does visualizing your success impact your motivation and confidence? Consider how incorporating visualization into your daily routine can help you stay focused and aligned with your aspirations.

Journal Prompt 2: Think of a challenge or obstacle you're currently facing in your life. Now, visualize yourself overcoming this challenge with grace and resilience. Picture yourself navigating through the difficulties with confidence and determination, emerging stronger on the other side. As you engage in this mental rehearsal, reflect on how it empowers you to confront obstacles with a positive mindset. How does visualizing your ability to overcome challenges influence your approach to problem-solving and adversity? Consider how integrating visualization techniques into your daily routine can enhance your resilience and foster personal growth.

SMALL CHANGE 13:
BOOSTING SELF-CONFIDENCE

"The moment you doubt whether you can fly,
you cease forever to be able to do it."

- J. M. BARRIE, PETER PAN

Self-confidence: Consider it as your inner strength, where you're fully confident in your abilities and judgment to tackle life's challenges with ease.

***

Picture yourself radiating with unstoppable confidence, ready to conquer any challenge that comes your way. In the previous chapter, we reviewed how visualization empowers us to proactively shape our future. Now, our journey leads us to explore another crucial element—boosting self-confidence—to unlock your fullest potential and sculpt your future success.

UNDERSTANDING THE ESSENCE OF SELF-CONFIDENCE:

Self-confidence, which many see as a key to doing well and feeling satisfied, is all about believing deeply in what you can do and how valuable you are. It's like having a strong inner well of bravery, toughness, and belief in yourself that helps you go after what you want in life.

Picture yourself radiating with unstoppable confidence, ready to conquer any challenge that comes your way. It's that unwavering belief in yourself, knowing deep down that you have what it takes to navigate life's twists and turns with grace and determination.

While some people seem to naturally have confidence, for many of us, building and keeping self-confidence is a journey of getting to know ourselves better and becoming stronger. It's about understanding what we're good at, accepting our differences, and believing in ourselves, even when things feel uncertain or tough.

Self-confidence isn't about being perfect or never experiencing fear or insecurity; it's about having the courage to step out of your comfort zone, take risks, and pursue your dreams with conviction and resilience, even when feeling fear or uncertainty.

RESEARCH AND INSIGHTS ON SELF-CONFIDENCE:

Ever wondered why some folks seem to handle life's ups and downs with ease while others struggle? Well, research from psychology and other fields gives us some clues about the power of self-confidence and how it shapes our journey through life.

Studies by Smith and Johnson (2018) and Lee et al. (2020) have demonstrated that individuals with greater self-confidence tend to set and pursue ambitious goals, persist in the face of challenges, and recover quickly from setbacks. Additionally, research conducted by Garcia (2019) and Patel et al. (2021) has highlighted the role of self-confidence in fostering positive self-esteem and overall well-being, empowering individuals to navigate life's challenges with a sense of agency and empowerment.

Research conducted by Bandura (1994) highlighted the role of self-efficacy, a key component of self-confidence, in shaping individuals' beliefs about their capabilities and influencing their behavior and achievements.

Furthermore, a longitudinal study published in the Journal of Applied Psychology found that self-confident individuals are more likely to experience career success and satisfaction, demonstrating the positive impact of self-confidence in professional settings (Judge & Bono, 2001). This study underscores the importance of self-confidence in achieving success and fulfillment in one's career.

In essence, research on self-confidence underscores its significance in various domains of life, from academic and professional success to interpersonal relationships and overall life satisfaction. By increasing their self-confidence, individuals can unlock their potential, embrace opportunities, and navigate life with greater courage and conviction.

THE MANY BENEFITS OF SELF-CONFIDENCE:

Self-confidence is another essential trait to have in our toolkit. It's like a helpful breeze nudging us along life's journey, bringing us all the good stuff that makes life better. To build and maintain self-confidence, we can start with small changes. Setting and achieving small goals boosts our sense of accomplishment. Positive self-talk can replace negative thoughts.

Surrounding ourselves with supportive people and celebrating our successes, no matter how small, can reinforce our self-belief. Let's dive into how building self-confidence helps us grow, feel good, and gives us a push in the right direction.

Here are some ways it makes our lives better:

Stronger Bounce-Back Ability: People with self-confidence can bounce back from tough times with strength and determination. Instead of feeling down or scared of failing, they see challenges as chances to learn and grow, pushing themselves closer to success.

Better Results: Self-confidence boosts performance by making people believe in their skills and potential. Whether it's in school, work, or personal goals, confident folks are more likely to aim high, work hard, and achieve impressive results.

Feeling Good About Yourself: Self-confidence helps you feel good about who you are. When you trust in yourself and what you can do, you shine with authenticity and inner strength, attracting others and forming meaningful bonds.

Speaking Up: Confident people speak up for themselves clearly and confidently, making sure their needs and boundaries are respected. By asserting themselves respectfully, they earn respect from others while staying true to their values.

More Happiness: Self-confidence is like a happiness booster. It gives you the power to chase your dreams, embrace opportunities, and live authentically. When you have faith in yourself, you move through life with purpose and passion, enjoying each moment with gratitude and joy.

Self-confidence is like a steady wind at our backs, propelling us forward through life's challenges and opportunities. It gives us the strength to bounce back from setbacks, perform at our best, and feel proud of who we are. With self-belief, we confidently assert ourselves and pursue our dreams, leading to a more fulfilling and joyful journey.

STRATEGIES FOR BOOSTING SELF-CONFIDENCE:

Building self-confidence might feel tricky sometimes, but it's totally doable with the right strategies. Check out these straightforward steps to boost your confidence and start feeling more empowered:

Be Kind to Yourself: Treat yourself with kindness and forgiveness, just like you would a friend. Embrace your flaws and mistakes as normal parts of being human – they don't define you!

Set Goals You Can Reach: Make goals that make sense for you and break them down into smaller steps. Celebrate every little win along the way – it'll help you see how capable you really are.

Kick Negative Thoughts to the Curb: Notice when you're being hard on yourself and challenge those negative thoughts. Replace them with positive affirmations that remind you of your worth and potential.

Embrace Learning and Growing: Look at challenges as chances to learn and grow. Stay curious and open-minded and tackle new experiences with excitement and resilience.

Speak Up for Yourself: Practice being assertive by speaking confidently and respectfully about what you need and want.

Use techniques like "I" statements and active listening to communicate clearly with others.

So, go ahead and give these tips a try—you've got this! Remember, building self-confidence is a journey, and every step you take is a win. Keep believing in yourself, and you'll be amazed at what you can achieve.

PRACTICAL APPLICATIONS OF SELF-CONFIDENCE IN DAILY LIFE:

Now that you've got some confidence-boosting tricks up your sleeve, let's see how they play out in your everyday adventures:

Better Relationships: When you believe in yourself, it's easier to be genuine and build trust with others. Having confidence helps you set healthy boundaries and speak up about what you need, which strengthens your connections. Imagine feeling comfortable expressing your thoughts and feelings without fear and being able to connect with others on a deeper level because you're confident in who you are.

Career Success: Confidence is a big factor in doing well at work. It gives you the courage to go after job opportunities, take risks, and show off your skills. Whether it's in job interviews, meetings, or networking, confidence helps you come across as capable and professional. Picture yourself confidently pitching your ideas in a meeting or breezing through a job interview because you believe in your abilities.

Personal Growth: Feeling confident encourages you to try new things and grow as a person. When you trust in yourself, you're more likely to pursue hobbies and interests that bring you joy and help you learn and grow. Imagine stepping out of your comfort zone to try new experiences and discover hidden talents because you believe in yourself.

Feeling Good Inside: Confidence isn't just about how you act—it also affects how you feel. When you have confidence, you're more resilient and at peace with yourself. You're less dependent on others' opinions and external circumstances to feel good about yourself. Envision feeling confident and content with who you are, regardless of what others think or what's happening around you.

Facing Challenges: Confidence gives you strength during tough times. When you believe in yourself, you can tackle obstacles with determination and grace, knowing you have what it takes to overcome them. Picture yourself facing challenges head-on, knowing that you have the inner strength and resilience to persevere, no matter what comes your way.

So go ahead, sprinkle a little confidence into your daily routine, and watch how it transforms your world into a playground of possibilities.

OVERCOMING SELF-DOUBT:

Self-doubt can be a big barrier to building self-confidence. Many of us struggle with doubting ourselves, feeling unsure and insecure, which holds us back from reaching our full potential. Overcoming this self-doubt is a journey of discovering who we are and feeling empowered, but it takes bravery, resilience, and being kind to ourselves.

One way to conquer self-doubt is by paying attention to your thoughts and feelings without being too critical. Understanding why you doubt yourselves helps you challenge those negative thoughts and build a mindset that's more positive and affirming.

Getting support from friends, family, or professionals can also make a big difference. Talking with someone who cares can offer guidance and encouragement, making it easier to believe in yourself and find your way forward. Whether it's chatting with a friend or seeking help from a therapist, having positive influences around you boosts your confidence and helps you bounce back from setbacks.

Being kind to yourself is key, too. Instead of being hard on yourself for making mistakes, it's important to treat yourself with kindness and remember that it's okay to mess up sometimes. Trying to be perfect all the time only adds to your self-doubt, so focusing on progress rather than perfection helps you grow and learn without feeling held back by doubt.

Personal Stories of Boosting Self-Confidence:

Let's examine two uplifting stories that show how boosting self-confidence can really make a difference in people's lives:

From Self-Doubt to Self-Assurance:

Alex, a recent college graduate, found himself grappling with self-doubt and insecurity as he embarked on his job search journey. Despite his qualifications and achievements, he harbored deep-seated fears of rejection and failure, constantly questioning his abilities and self-worth.

However, Alex refused to let his doubts define him. Through mentorship and dedicated self-reflection, he embarked on a journey to challenge his negative self-talk and break free from limiting beliefs. With each introspective session, Alex gradually began to recognize and appreciate his strengths and past accomplishments, slowly but steadily building his confidence from within.

But Alex didn't stop there. He actively sought out networking opportunities, engaged in rigorous interview practice sessions, and eagerly participated in professional development workshops. By immersing himself in these experiences, he not only honed his skills but also gained valuable insights into his own capabilities, reinforcing his growing sense of self-assurance.

As he navigated the competitive job market armed with his newfound confidence, Alex's efforts bore fruit. He secured a fulfilling job opportunity that resonated deeply with his passions and aspirations, validating his belief in himself and his abilities. Through his arduous journey of nurturing self-confidence, Alex not only attained employment but also cultivated a profound sense of self-awareness and empowerment that would continue to propel him forward in his future endeavors.

Journey to Authenticity:

Emily, a young woman filled with dreams and aspirations, often felt a heavy weight of uncertainty weighing her down as she journeyed through life. Despite her inner strength, doubts about her abilities and questions about where she belonged clouded her mind.

Yet, Emily refused to let these doubts define her. With courage in her heart, she set out on a journey to find herself and build her confidence. She confided in her supportive friends, leaned on her family for encouragement, and sought advice from mentors who had walked similar paths.

Through this brave journey of opening up and being true to herself, Emily started to unravel the layers of doubt that had held her back for so long. She began to see her vulnerabilities as strengths and embraced them as part of who she was.

With each small step forward, Emily's confidence grew. She explored activities that sparked joy in her heart, such as painting, hiking in nature, and volunteering in her community. These experiences helped her discover her passions and gave her a sense of purpose.

As Emily continued to embrace her true self and pursue her dreams with determination, she found a sense of fulfillment that she had never experienced before. Her journey taught her that being authentic and staying true to herself was the key to unlocking a life of happiness and contentment.

Emily's story serves as an inspiration to others who may be struggling with self-doubt and uncertainty. It shows that with courage and perseverance, it's possible to overcome obstacles and find your authentic place in the world, no matter how daunting the journey may seem.

IN A NUTSHELL:

On our path to self-confidence, we've discovered how it shapes our response to life's challenges. Through self-discovery, acts of kindness, and the courage to speak up, you grow a strong belief in yourself. Instead of feeling unsure or overwhelmed, you find the courage to face difficulties head-on and navigate life with purpose and determination.

We've also learned how to deal with doubts and fears. It's normal to feel unsure sometimes, but with effort, you can overcome these feelings. Stories like Alex's and Emily's show us that even when we doubt ourselves, we can still achieve great things. As we keep growing and learning, let's remember that building confidence takes time. But every step you take brings you closer to living your best life.

CONTINUING EDUCATION RESOURCES FOR BOOSTING SELF-CONFIDENCE:

1. *The Confidence Code: The Science and Art of Self-Assurance—What Women Should Know* by Katty Kay and Claire Shipman
2. *Self-Confidence: The Remarkable Truth of Why a Small Change Can Make a Big Difference* by Paul McGee
3. *The Gifts of Imperfection: Let Go of Who You Think You're Supposed to Be and Embrace Who You Are* by Brené Brown
4. *Feel the Fear... and Do It Anyway* by Susan Jeffers
5. *You Are a Badass: How to Stop Doubting Your Greatness and Start Living an Awesome Life* by Jen Sincero

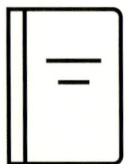

JOURNALING PROMPTS FOR BOOSTING SELF-CONFIDENCE:

Journaling prompts are a great way to help you engage with the material and reflect on your own experiences. Here are two prompts for this chapter:

Journal Prompt 1: Reflect on a recent accomplishment or success in your life, big or small. How did your self-confidence play a role in achieving this goal? Consider how believing in yourself and your abilities helped you navigate challenges, stay focused on your objectives, and ultimately achieve success. Write about the emotions you experienced throughout the process and how they influenced your journey toward accomplishing your goal.

Journal Prompt 2: Think about a situation in which you felt doubt or insecurity about yourself or your abilities. What thoughts or beliefs contributed to these feelings of self-doubt? Reflect on how you typically respond to moments of doubt and uncertainty. Then, consider strategies you could use to nurture your self-confidence and challenge negative self-talk in similar situations in the future. Write about how you can cultivate a mindset of self-assurance and resilience to overcome self-doubt and pursue your goals with confidence.

SMALL CHANGE 14: MASTERING HABITS AND ROUTINES

"The secret of your future is hidden in your daily routine."

- MIKE MURDOCK

Habits: Think of them as the small actions we repeat every day that can either move us forward toward our goals or hold us back.

***

"I bought a ton of self-help books and started investing in myself. Want to know what I discovered? The happiest, healthiest, and wealthiest people in the world have one thing in common. They have routines they follow, especially morning routines that set them up for successful days, weeks, months, years, and lives." These are the words of author Mary Sciglimpaglia Brainard, written in her book *Get Up, Get Going.*

In this chapter, as we tackle life's challenges with resilience and work toward self-improvement, we'll see how our daily habits and routines deeply influence our lives. They help us overcome obstacles, stay productive, and grow personally. Building on our previous discussion about the benefits of self-confidence, we'll also explore how these habits can help us overcome self-doubt and build confidence, giving us the strength to face life with more certainty and authenticity.

THE SIGNIFICANCE OF HABITS AND ROUTINES:

Did you know that the stuff you do every morning, like whether you exercise, have breakfast, or scroll through social media, can set the tone for your whole day? Those actions are your morning habits. They can affect your mood, energy levels, and productivity all day long.

Habits and routines are like the building blocks of your life. They're the things you do without really thinking about them, but they have a big impact on how your days, weeks, and even years turn out. From the way you brush your teeth to the way you organize your day, habits and routines shape the fabric of your existence, underscoring their significance in determining the quality of our lives.

Understanding why habits and routines matter can help you make them work for you in all aspects of your life, not just in the morning. Whether it's the way you approach work, how you interact with others, or how you spend your leisure time, your habits and routines play a role in shaping your experiences.

By being mindful of the habits you've developed and actively choosing ones that align with your goals and values, you can create a more fulfilling and purpose-driven life. So, whether it's establishing a bedtime routine to improve your sleep quality or incorporating regular exercise into your week, every small change adds up to a big impact on your overall well-being and happiness.

RESEARCH AND INSIGHTS ON HABITS AND ROUTINES:

A wealth of research and insights from psychology, neuroscience, and behavioral science sheds light on the intricate mechanisms underlying habits and routines. According to studies by Duhigg (2012) and Clear (2018), habits are formed through a process of repetition and reinforcement, wherein behaviors become automatic and ingrained through consistent practice.

Moreover, research on habit formation highlights the role of cues, routines, and rewards in shaping our behavioral patterns. As outlined in a study by Wood and Neal (2007); by identifying the triggers that prompt certain behaviors, implementing consistent routines, and rewarding ourselves for positive actions, we can cultivate new habits and break free from old ones.

In essence, research on habits and routines underscores their profound impact on our behavior, cognition, and overall well-being. According to a study by Lyubomirsky (2008), by mastering habits and routines, we can harness their power to create positive change and achieve our goals with greater efficiency and effectiveness.

EXPLORING THE BENEFITS OF MASTERING HEALTHY HABITS AND ROUTINES:

Mastering healthy habits and routines brings us a bunch of perks that make life better. Let's check out some of these benefits from the angle of personal growth and feeling fulfilled:

Get More Done: When we have good habits and routines, we use our time and energy better, so we can finish tasks easier and quicker. For example, imagine having a morning routine where you always make your bed, eat a healthy breakfast, and plan out your day.

This sets you up with a positive mindset and helps you tackle tasks more efficiently throughout the day. Similarly, having a structured work routine, like breaking tasks into smaller steps or scheduling specific times for focused work, can make it easier to stay productive and get more done.

Improved Health and Well-Being: Habits and routines play a crucial role in promoting physical and mental health. From regular exercise and balanced nutrition to mindfulness practices and self-care rituals, acquiring healthy habits and routines improves our well-being and vitality.

By making healthy choices a regular part of our daily routines, we boost our energy levels, strengthen our immune systems, and improve our mood. For instance, going for a walk or practicing yoga each day can enhance physical fitness and reduce stress, while preparing nutritious meals and getting enough sleep support overall health and resilience.

Greater Consistency and Discipline: Mastering habits and routines instills discipline and consistency in our lives, empowering us to stay on track toward our goals and aspirations. By committing to daily rituals and practices, we cultivate resilience and perseverance, overcoming obstacles with determination and grit.

For example, setting aside specific times each day for tasks such as studying, exercising, or working on personal projects helps us maintain focus and progress steadily toward our objectives.

Enhanced Focus and Clarity: Habits and routines create structure and order in our lives, reducing decision fatigue and mental clutter. By automating repetitive tasks and establishing clear routines, we free up mental space and bandwidth, allowing us to focus on what truly matters and pursue our priorities with clarity and purpose.

For instance, having a morning routine where you follow the same steps each day—like exercising, showering, and having breakfast—helps you start the day smoothly without having to think too much about what to do next. This clarity and simplicity in your routine can carry over to other aspects of your day, helping you stay focused and productive.

Heightened Sense of Control: Mastering habits and routines enables us to take control of our lives and destinies. By intentionally shaping our behaviors and environments, we cultivate a sense of agency and autonomy, allowing us to navigate life's complexities with confidence and resilience.

For example, having a bedtime routine where you disconnect from electronic devices and engage in relaxing activities like reading or meditation can help you feel more in control of your sleep patterns and overall well-being. This sense of control extends beyond just your bedtime routine— it spills over into other areas of your life, like your relationships, work, and hobbies. This helps you make decisions that match what you believe in and what you want to achieve.

Building healthy habits and routines can seriously level up your life. You get more done, feel better, and stay on track with your goals. It's all about setting yourself up for success, whether that's through a killer morning routine, staying active, eating right, or sticking to a schedule. Give it a try, and watch how these small changes can make a big difference!

STRATEGIES FOR MASTERING HABITS AND ROUTINES:

While habits and routines may appear difficult to change initially, they can be adjusted and improved with intentional effort and practice.

Here are some practical strategies for mastering habits and routines to facilitate positive change in your life:

Start Small: Let's say you want to start exercising regularly. Instead of aiming to run a marathon right away, you could begin by committing to a 10-minute walk every morning or doing a quick yoga session before bed. These small changes are easier to stick to and can gradually lead to bigger habits like going to the gym or training for a race.

Set Clear Goals: Imagine you want to improve your productivity at work. You could set a clear goal to finish responding to all your emails by 11 a.m. each day. When you think about how finishing your emails early helps you be less stressed and more organized for the rest of your day, it gives you a clear motivation to stick to your new routine.

Create Rituals and Cues: Consider if you want to drink more water throughout the day. You could establish a ritual of filling up a water bottle first thing in the morning and placing it on your desk as a visual cue. Whenever you see the water bottle, it reminds you to take a sip, gradually building the habit of staying hydrated.

Track Your Progress: Let's say you're working on spending less time on your phone before bed to improve your sleep.

You could use a habit tracker app to keep an eye on how many hours you're scrolling each night. By acknowledging and celebrating each night that you successfully reduce your screen time, you'll feel motivated to keep making progress.

Practice Self-Reflection: Picture yourself eating healthier meals. You could take some time each week to reflect on your eating habits, noting which meals were balanced and satisfying and which ones could use improvement. By being honest with yourself about your choices, you can identify patterns and make adjustments to support not only your health goals but also other areas of your life where you want to see positive changes.

Remember, by incorporating these strategies into your daily routine and staying committed to positive change, you'll be well on your way to building healthier habits and achieving your goals. So, keep at it, stay focused, and watch how these simple tweaks can lead to big wins in your life!

OVERCOMING RESISTANCE AND ESTABLISHING NEW HABITS:

Despite the many benefits of mastering habits and routines, many people find it tough to get started or stick with them. Overcoming that resistance and inertia takes patience, determination, and a healthy dose of self-compassion. It also requires a willingness to experiment and try new approaches.

But don't worry! I've got some clever strategies to help you out. Remember those handy tricks we talked about earlier? Well, they're not just for show—they can work wonders for all kinds of improvements in life. So whether you're starting small, teaming up for accountability, or simply being more mindful, these methods can really boost your journey to a better you.

Stick to your guns, stay focused on your goals, and watch how these simple tweaks can lead to big wins in your life:

Small Steps: One effective approach for overcoming resistance and establishing new habits is to start small and build momentum gradually. Focus on making incremental changes and celebrating small wins along the way, rather than trying to overhaul your entire routine overnight. By breaking down your goals into manageable steps and setting realistic expectations, you create a pathway for success and sustainable change.

Accountability Buddies: Additionally, creating accountability and support systems can provide motivation and encouragement as you work toward establishing new habits. Whether it's enlisting the support of a friend, joining a group or community with similar goals, or working with a coach or mentor, surrounding yourself with positive influences and resources can help you stay motivated and committed to your habits and routines.

Mindful Practices: Incorporating mindfulness practices such as meditation, visualization, and deep breathing can also help overcome resistance and cultivate a more open and receptive mindset. By cultivating present-moment awareness and self-compassion, you can navigate challenges and setbacks with grace and resilience, staying focused on your long-term goals and aspirations.

As we work on mastering our habits and routines, it's normal to feel scared or stuck when we try to change. Overcoming these challenges just takes time, sticking with it, and being kind to yourself. It's okay to try new things and adjust as you go. Think of it like learning to ride a bike – it might be tricky at first, but with practice, you'll get better.

Each time you push through, you learn more about yourself and get stronger. So, keep going, and you'll find yourself living a more fulfilling and purposeful life.

PERSONAL STORIES OF MASTERING HABITS AND ROUTINES:

Let's explore two instances that illustrate the power of mastering habits and routines:

From Procrastination to Productivity:

Meet Mia, a single mom in her 30s juggling a job and taking care of her kids. She's been feeling overwhelmed by all the demands on her time and energy. Despite her best intentions, she struggles to stay focused and organized, often finding herself putting off important tasks until the last minute.

But Mia refuses to let procrastination hold her back. She starts digging into what's behind her tendency to delay things and experiments with different strategies to overcome it. She decides to create a structured daily schedule, breaking down her responsibilities into smaller, more manageable chunks and setting aside specific times for work and family.

To keep herself accountable, Mia starts tracking her progress and rewarding herself for sticking to her plan. It's not easy at first, but she's determined to make it work. As she sticks to her new routine and develops better habits, she begins to see a real difference in how much she's able to accomplish.

With her newfound sense of control, Mia not only meets her work deadlines and keeps up with her kids' schedules but also starts to feel more confident and empowered in other areas of her life. By tackling her procrastination head-on, she's able to create a brighter future for herself and her family.

Embracing Mindful Living:

Meet James, a guy in his late 40s with a lot on his plate. He's balancing a demanding job as a project manager, where deadlines are always looming, with the responsibilities of being a father to two energetic kids and a husband to a spouse who's also managing a career.

On top of that, James is involved in his community, volunteering at his kids' school and coaching their soccer team. He's also trying to stay healthy by squeezing in workouts at the gym a few times a week, all while managing household chores and errands.

With so much going on, James feels like he's constantly racing against the clock. Despite his best efforts to stay organized, he often finds himself feeling overwhelmed and drained, struggling to find time for himself amidst the chaos of daily life.

But James isn't giving up just yet. He starts trying out this thing called mindful living, which is all about being more aware and present in your everyday life. He gives meditation a shot, takes some deep breaths, and tries doing some mindful movements to find moments of calm in the middle of the chaos.

And you know what? As James gets more into this mindful living stuff, things start to change for him in a big way. He begins to see things differently and starts focusing on what's really important to him. He learns to deal with his thoughts and feelings better, facing challenges with patience and kindness instead of getting all worked up. Plus, he starts appreciating the little things in life more, finding happiness in simple stuff.

By sticking to these new habits and routines, James not only gets better at handling his busy life and feeling more relaxed, but he also finds a deeper sense of meaning and happiness. By embracing mindful living, he learns to stay calm and true to himself, no matter what life throws his way.

In a Nutshell:

In the end, getting better at habits and routines involves making a few small changes where we learn a lot about ourselves and feel more in control. By practicing things like mindfulness, setting clear goals, and being consistent, we can use habits and routines to make our lives better and reach our goals faster and easier.

Establishing consistent morning routines can have a profound impact on our overall well-being and success. By starting each day with intentionality and mindfulness, we set a positive tone for the rest of the day. These morning rituals not only help us to feel more grounded and focused, but they also lay the foundation for successful days, weeks, months, and even years ahead. By prioritizing self-care and setting positive intentions each morning, we can create a ripple effect of productivity, fulfillment, and happiness throughout our lives.

Next, we'll explore the power of intention—being crystal clear about where we're headed with our actions. We'll see how setting clear intentions helps us stay on track and keeps us pumped up, backed by research. Plus, we'll figure out how to match our intentions with what really counts, so we can use intention to make our lives even better.

But first, be sure to check out the additional resources to learn more about habits and routines.

CONTINUING EDUCATION RESOURCES FOR MASTERING HABITS AND ROUTINES:

1. *Atomic Habits: An Easy & Proven Way to Build Good Habits & Break Bad Ones* by James Clear
2. *The Power of Habit: Why We Do What We Do in Life and Business* by Charles Duhigg
3. *Tiny Habits: The Small Changes That Change Everything* by BJ Fogg
4. *Daily Rituals: How Artists Work* by Mason Currey
5. *The Miracle Morning: The Not-So-Obvious Secret Guaranteed to Transform Your Life (Before 8 AM)* by Hal Elrod

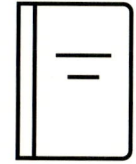

JOURNALING PROMPTS FOR MASTERING HABITS AND ROUTINES:

Journaling prompts are a great way to help you engage with the material and reflect on your own experiences. Here are two prompts for this chapter:

Journal Prompt 1: Reflect on your current daily habits and routines. Which ones do you feel contribute positively to your life, and which ones do you think could be improved or changed? Consider how these habits impact your mood, energy levels, productivity, and overall well-being. Write about any adjustments you would like to make and how you plan to implement them to create a more fulfilling daily routine.

Journal Prompt 2: Think about a time when you successfully established a new habit or routine in your life. What motivated you to make this change, and how did you go about implementing it? Reflect on any challenges you faced along the way and how you overcame them. Consider the benefits you experienced as a result of this new habit or routine and how it has impacted your life positively. Write about the lessons you learned from this experience and how you can apply them to future habit-building endeavors.

SMALL CHANGE 15:
LIVING WITH INTENTION

"An unintentional life accepts everything and does nothing. An intentional life embraces only the things that will add to the mission of significance."

- JOHN C. MAXWELL

Intention: It's like your game plan—what you're aiming for and how you're going to get there. Living with intention means building your life around what really matters to you, being cool with who you are, and understanding that it's okay to make mistakes along the way.

***

Living an intentional life means that the way you choose to spend your time and the decisions you make are all in service to the purpose you have set for your life. That's what intention is about. It's what drives our actions, shaping where we're going. Living with intention means being clear about our goals and making choices that lead us there. It's what helps us work better, feel happier, and enjoy life more.

THE MEANING OF LIVING WITH INTENTION:

Living with intention means being purposeful and mindful in what we do. It's like having a plan for what we want to achieve. It guides our decisions and helps us reach our dreams. This deliberate approach to life allows us to focus our energy on the things that truly matter to us, rather than getting caught up in distractions or going with the flow without direction.

Understanding this is important because it can bring good changes to your life. When you live with intention, it's like you're the architect of your own life. You set clear goals and figure out how to achieve them. Every thought, feeling, and action you have fits with your plan, moving you closer to your goals. This way of living helps you make smart choices and do things that make you happy.

It's about staying true to who you are and making the most of each day. By embracing this idea, you can make significant changes in your life. Are you ready to start living with intention and make your dreams come true? Ensuring your actions align with your biggest dreams and hopes? That's what putting intention into action is all about.

RESEARCH AND INSIGHTS ON INTENTIONAL LIVING:

Research According to studies by renowned researchers like Dweck (2006) and Gollwitzer (1999), setting clear intentions activates specific neural networks in the brain associated with goal-directed behavior. These findings suggest that when we establish clear intentions, our brain becomes more focused and motivated, increasing our likelihood of persisting toward achieving our goals.

Furthermore, research by Emmons and McCullough (2003) highlights the significance of aligning our thoughts, emotions, and actions with our core values and aspirations. By gaining a clear sense of purpose and directing our energy toward meaningful objectives, we can use intention to drive positive change and fulfillment in our lives.

Additionally, Lyubomirsky, Sheldon, and Schkade (2005) explored the relationship between intentional activities and happiness, concluding that individuals who engage in intentional behaviors aimed at increasing their well-being, such as expressing gratitude or practicing acts of kindness, often experience a significant boost in their overall happiness levels. This research underscores the importance of intentionally directing our actions toward activities that promote well-being and fulfillment.

In essence, studies on intentional living underscore its significant impact on behavior, cognition, and overall well-being (Dweck, 2006; Gollwitzer, 1999; Emmons & McCullough, 2003). By putting intentional living practices into action, such as setting clear intentions and aligning actions with values, we can tap into its potential to promote purpose, passion, and fulfillment across all areas of our lives.

EXPLORING THE BENEFITS OF LIVING WITH INTENTION:

Living with intention brings a bunch of great stuff into our lives, making things clearer, sharper, and more fulfilling. It paves the way for increased happiness, productivity, and overall well-being, ensuring that each day is lived with purpose and satisfaction.

Let's check out some of these awesome benefits:

Clarity of Purpose: Living with intention helps us figure out what really matters to us. By setting clear intentions, we get a better grip on our values, priorities, and dreams. This clarity guides us toward making choices that align with what we truly want in life.

Enhanced Focus and Concentration: Intention acts like a spotlight, helping us zero in on what we want to achieve and avoid wasting time on distractions. By focusing our energy and attention on our goals, we stay on track and make progress toward success and fulfillment.

Increased Motivation and Persistence: Living with intention gives us a boost of energy and determination to keep going, even when things get tough. By knowing exactly what we're aiming for and visualizing our success, we stay motivated and don't give up easily.

Greater Resilience and Adaptability: Intention helps us bounce back from challenges and adapt to changes. By staying true to our values and goals, we build up inner strength and flexibility, allowing us to roll with the punches and keep moving forward.

Enhanced Self-Awareness and Self-Empowerment: Living with intention helps us understand ourselves better and take charge of our lives. By being mindful and intentional in what we do, we become the bosses of our own destiny, shaping our reality with confidence and purpose.

Living with intention isn't just about going through the motions—it's about living a life that's truly meaningful and fulfilling. By aligning our actions with our values and dreams, we can experience a deeper sense of purpose and satisfaction. Intentionality encourages us to make conscious choices and take deliberate steps toward the life we want to live. It's about recognizing that every decision we make shapes our reality and being proactive in creating the future we envision.

So, whether it's pursuing a passion, nurturing relationships, or striving for personal growth, living with intention empowers us to live our best lives, one intentional choice at a time.

STRATEGIES FOR LIVING WITH INTENTION:

Living with intention might feel a bit tricky at first, but it's totally doable with some practice. It's about taking control of your life and steering it in the direction you want to go. By incorporating intentional living strategies into your daily routine, you can unlock a deeper sense of purpose and fulfillment.

Here are some simple tips to get you started on living with intention and making big, positive changes in your life:

Stay Present: Pay more attention to your thoughts, feelings, and actions throughout the day. Try out stuff like meditation or just taking a moment to breathe deeply. This helps you figure out what you really want and why.

Set Goals: Take some time to figure out exactly what you want to achieve and why it's important to you. Write it down in a journal or create a vision board to help you see your goals clearly.

Picture Success: Imagine yourself reaching your goals and living the life you dream of. Picture it in your mind, thinking about how it feels, sounds, and looks. This can keep you motivated and focused on your goals.

Take Small Steps: Break your goals into smaller, manageable steps and start taking action toward them. Stay open to new opportunities and trust that you're moving in the right direction, even if things don't always go as planned.

Appreciate the Good: Take time to notice and be thankful for the good things in your life and the progress you've made toward your goals. Being grateful can help you stay positive and attract even more good stuff into your life.

Living with intention is like navigating through a maze with a clear map—challenging but totally worth it. By embracing mindfulness, setting goals, visualizing success, taking gradual steps, and practicing gratitude, you're not just living; you're crafting a life that's uniquely yours. Give it a shot, and you'll see the magic unfold. Remember, every small step you take towards intentional living brings you closer to a life filled with meaning and joy.

PRACTICAL APPLICATIONS OF LIVING WITH INTENTION IN DAILY LIFE:

Now that we've talked about living with intention along with some tips to get you started, let's explore how we can integrate these concepts into our everyday routines for a more purposeful and fulfilling life. From goal setting to relationship building, decision making to self-care, living with intention offers practical applications that can transform the way we navigate our daily lives.

Here are some simple tips to help you kickstart this journey:

Set Clear Goals: Figure out what you want and how to get there. For example, if you want to improve your health, commit to exercising for 30 minutes, five days a week. Plan your workouts and prepare healthy meals to support your goal.

Make Smart Choices: Use intention to guide your decisions and solve problems confidently. When faced with a tough decision, think about your long-term goals and values. This helps you make choices that align with what's important to you.

Strengthen Connections: Get closer to the people around you by being intentional in your conversations. Listen carefully, show you care, and let them know how you want to connect. This helps build trust and makes your relationships stronger.

Take Me-Time Seriously: Make sure you're taking care of yourself. Set aside some time each day for activities like meditation or relaxation. It's important for keeping your mood balanced and your spirits up.

Spread the Good Vibes: Give back and make a positive impact in your community. Look for ways to help out that match your values. Whether it's volunteering or lending a hand to someone in need, every little bit helps.

By putting these practical ideas into action in our daily lives, we can live with more clarity, purpose, and happiness, getting closer to our goals and dreams. Remember, every small step taken with intention has the power to create positive change, not only in our own lives but also in the lives of those around us. So, let's embrace intentional living as a guiding principle and watch as it enriches every aspect of our daily existence.

OVERCOMING CHALLENGES AND BUILDING RESILIENCE:

Even though living with intention can bring lots of good stuff, sometimes we might face resistance and obstacles along the way. Overcoming these challenges and building resilience takes time, patience, and showing ourselves compassion, as well as being open to change and learning new things.

One way to tackle challenges and build resilience is by showing ourselves kindness and accepting who we are. It's important to treat ourselves with understanding, knowing that it's normal to face setbacks and tough times as we grow and discover ourselves. By approaching challenges with an open heart and mind, we can become stronger and more adaptable when things get tough.

Also, having supportive people around us and seeking advice from mentors and coaches can make a big difference. Connecting with others who share our values and goals can give us the encouragement and guidance we need to keep going, even when things feel tough.

And don't forget about mindfulness practices like meditation and journaling. These can help us stay grounded and focused, even when life throws us curveballs. By being present and accepting of whatever comes our way, we can face challenges with grace and strength, knowing that our intentions and goals will guide us through.

PERSONAL STORIES OF IMPLEMENTING INTENTION:

Let's explore two inspiring anecdotes that show how living with intention can change lives for the better:

Turning Dreams into Reality:

Aisha was more than just an artist; she was a dreamer with a vision that seemed too big for her to grasp. Her heart overflowed with passion for her craft, but a cloud of self-doubt loomed over her aspirations. The idea of showcasing her artwork in a prestigious gallery ignited a spark within her, yet the fear of rejection and failure dimmed its glow.

Despite the shadows that threatened to engulf her dreams, Aisha dared to embrace the practice of living with intention. With each stroke of her brush, she breathed life into her vision, infusing it with clarity and conviction. Setting clear intentions became her beacon in the storm of uncertainty, guiding her through the labyrinth of self-doubt.

As Aisha poured her heart and soul into her art, she saw beyond the canvas, envisioning herself standing proudly in a gallery adorned with her creations. The mere thought of sharing her passion with the world fueled her determination to push past her fears. With each step she took toward her dream, she felt the weight of doubt gradually lift from her shoulders, replaced by a sense of purpose and empowerment.

Alongside her intentions, Aisha cultivated a support system that lifted her up when doubts threatened to pull her down. Encouragement from fellow artists and guidance from mentors provided her with the strength and resilience to weather the storms of uncertainty. Through their unwavering support, Aisha found solace in the knowledge that she was not alone in her journey.

Despite the many challenges and obstacles that littered her path, Aisha remained focused on the pursuit of her dreams. With unwavering determination, she persevered, believing in the power of living with intention. And as she stood in that gallery, surrounded by the fruits of her labor, Aisha knew that her journey was not just about fulfilling a dream—it was about knowing and living her true purpose and finding fulfillment in the process.

A Journey of Intention and Growth:

Elias felt stuck in a rut at his job. He hadn't achieved much and felt lost, unsure of what to do next. But then he came across this idea called living with intention. It sounded hopeful, like a light in the dark. Setting intentions became his guide, showing him a way forward.

With this new idea in mind, Elias decided to figure out what really mattered to him. He started trying out different things, like helping out in his community and exploring hobbies outside of work, hoping to find something that made him excited and happy. He found that volunteering at a local shelter and painting in his spare time brought him joy and purpose, giving him a sense of fulfillment that was missing in his job.

As Elias started aligning his actions with his intentions, he felt a change inside. He began to feel more motivated and purposeful, like he was finally moving forward. Each small step he took made him feel proud and encouraged him to keep going, even when things got tough. He started setting small goals for himself at work, like completing tasks ahead of schedule or taking on new projects that interested him, which boosted his confidence and made him feel more engaged in his job.

With the support of people who believed in him, Elias found the courage to push past his doubts and try new things. Despite the challenges he faced, he kept going, determined to live with intention and find meaning in his work. He started seeking out mentors and networking with colleagues who shared his passions, which helped him gain valuable insights and grow professionally.

Standing at a crossroads, Elias knew he had a clear path ahead of him—a path lit up by intention, where progress was possible, and a brighter future awaited. He felt more hopeful and optimistic about his career than ever before, knowing that he had the power to create a fulfilling and meaningful work life for himself.

IN A NUTSHELL:

Living with intention is like having a compass for your life. It's about figuring out what really matters to you and then making choices that move you closer to those things. By setting intentions, we're basically telling ourselves what we want to achieve and why it's important to us. And when we align our thoughts and actions with our intentions, we're more likely to see positive changes happen in our lives.

Living with intention isn't about trying to control everything or forcing things to happen. It's about being open to new opportunities and trusting that we're moving in the right direction, even if things don't always go as planned. It's about being present in the moment and making the most out of every experience, knowing that each step we take is bringing us closer to the life we want.

***

Congratulations on completing the fifteen small changes! You've taken a big step toward living a more mindful, meaningful life. Each one is like a valuable piece of a puzzle, helping you unlock greater happiness and fulfillment. But remember, you'll need to put in the effort to fully benefit from each strategy.

Now, let's talk about how you can implement and benefit from these small changes to lead to big results in your life. Think of each small change as a building block for personal growth and lasting happiness. By incorporating these strategies into your daily routine and mindset, you're laying the foundation for a more fulfilling life.

First, it's essential to approach each small change with intention and commitment. Take the time to understand why you're making the change and how it aligns with your goals and values. By being intentional in your actions, you'll be more likely to stick with them and see positive results over time.

Next, embrace the power of consistency. Small changes may seem insignificant on their own, but when practiced consistently over time, they can lead to significant improvements in your life. Make a commitment to yourself to stick with each change, even when it feels challenging or you encounter setbacks along the way.

Additionally, be patient with yourself and celebrate your progress along the journey. Personal growth takes time, and it's normal to experience ups and downs along the way. Instead of focusing on perfection, focus on progress and the positive changes you're making in your life.

Finally, remember that these small changes aren't just about reaching a destination; they're about enjoying the journey. Take time to reflect on how each change is impacting your life and bringing you closer to your goals. By staying present and appreciating the process, you'll find greater joy and fulfillment in every step you take.

So, keep up the great work, and continue to embrace these small changes as opportunities for growth and transformation in your life. With dedication and perseverance, you'll unlock a world of possibilities and create the life you've always dreamed of.

And hey, if you've read my other books, you know I like to give you extra goodies to help you live your best life. So, in the next part, we're diving into how taking care of your body can make your mind and spirit thrive. It's all about simple habits that can make a big difference in how you feel every day. Get ready for some easy small changes to help you feel happier and healthier than ever!

CONTINUING EDUCATION RESOURCES FOR LIVING WITH INTENTION:

1. *The Power of Intention: Learning to Co-create Your World Your Way* by Wayne W. Dyer
2. *Intention: Critical Creativity in the Classroom* by Amy Burvall and Dan Ryder
3. *Living with Intent: My Somewhat Messy Journey to Purpose, Peace, and Joy* by Mallika Chopra
4. *The Intention Experiment: Using Your Thoughts to Change Your Life and the World* by Lynne McTaggart
5. *Master Your Mindpower: A User Manual For Your Mind & The Ultimate Guide To Mental Toughness:* by Stéphane Schafeitel

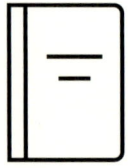

JOURNALING PROMPTS FOR LIVING WITH INTENTION:

Journaling prompts are a great way to help you engage with the material and reflect on your own experiences. Here are two prompts for this chapter:

Journal Prompt 1: Reflect on your current approach to living with intention. How often do you consciously align your actions with your core beliefs and values? Consider specific areas of your life where you could be more intentional, such as your career, relationships, personal development, or self-care practices. Write about any changes you would like to make to live more intentionally and how you plan to incorporate them into your daily life.

Journal Prompt 2: Think about a time when you achieved a significant goal or experienced a meaningful outcome as a result of living with intention. What steps did you take to set clear intentions and align your actions with your goals? Reflect on any challenges you faced along the way and how you overcame them with patience, resilience, and self-compassion. Write about the lessons you learned from this experience and how you can apply them to other areas of your life where you want to live more intentionally.

BONUS 1: ADOPTING HEALTHY LIVING HABITS

"Good health is not something we can buy. However, it can be an extremely valuable savings account."

- ANNE WILSON SCHAEF

Healthy living: It's all about doing things that make us healthier. It's the actions we take to keep ourselves in top shape. It's a lifestyle that helps us avoid serious illness or premature death. It's not just about avoiding sickness; it's about feeling great in body, mind, and heart.

***

Congratulations on reaching this point and putting in the effort to apply what you've learned! It's no small feat, but you're doing great. So far, we've explored a bunch of small changes—15, to be exact—to help boost your happiness and resilience on your path to improving your life. We've discussed how to handle setbacks and keep moving toward our goals. But remember, putting these ideas into action is an ongoing effort. Never giving up on your dream is a lifelong journey.

So, let's keep going. Taking care of your body and mind is another key to living a healthier, happier, and fulfilling life. In this first of two extra chapters, we'll dive into simple ways to support your physical, mental, and social well-being.

NOURISHING YOUR BODY:

First, let's talk about something crucial: healthy eating. You've probably heard the saying, "You are what you eat," and it holds true. Fueling your body with nutritious foods that give you energy and vitality is essential. Imagine starting your day with a colorful breakfast bowl packed with fruits, whole grains, and a dollop of yogurt.

Throughout the day, focus on incorporating plenty of fruits, vegetables, whole grains, and lean proteins into your meals. It's about finding a balance that works for you, nourishing your body with the fuel it needs to thrive. Don't forget to stay hydrated by drinking plenty of water and try to limit your intake of processed foods and sugary drinks.

Nourishing your body with healthy eating habits offers a myriad of benefits beyond just energy and vitality. By fueling yourself with nutrient-rich foods, you can also reduce the risk of various health issues such as heart disease, diabetes, and obesity. Additionally, healthy eating can help improve digestion, reducing discomforts like acid indigestion and bloating.

Furthermore, maintaining a balanced diet can enhance cognitive function, sharpening your focus and memory. By prioritizing wholesome foods like fruits, vegetables, whole grains, and lean proteins, you're not only nourishing your body but also safeguarding your long-term health and well-being.

So, as you progress on your journey toward a healthier lifestyle, remember the profound impact that healthy eating can have on every aspect of your life.

Now, let's take a closer look at Kate's journey to better health through nutrition. Like many of us, Kate used to rely on fast food and sugary snacks to get her through the day. However, she always felt tired and sluggish, struggling to find the energy to tackle her daily tasks.

Determined to make a change, she started incorporating more fruits, vegetables, and whole grains into her diet. Instead of reaching for a candy bar in the afternoon, she opted for a piece of fruit or a handful of nuts. As a result of these small changes, Kate noticed a remarkable difference in how she felt.

Her energy levels soared, her mood improved, and she experienced better overall health. Inspired by her success, she continued to make healthier choices, ultimately transforming her lifestyle for the better.

By prioritizing foods like fruits, vegetables, whole grains, and lean proteins, you're providing your body with the essential nutrients it needs to thrive. Remember to stay hydrated and limit your intake of processed foods and sugary drinks. As we move forward, let's keep these healthy eating habits in mind as part of our overall journey toward a healthier, happier life.

GET MOVING:

Exercise isn't just about staying fit; it's also great for your mind and mood. Regular physical activity can have numerous benefits, including reducing stress, improving sleep, and boosting mood. Find things you like doing and do them often. It could be taking walks in nature, dancing at home, or doing yoga in the park. These activities help your body release feel-good chemicals.

Meet John. He dealt with feeling sad and worried for a long time until he found out how helpful exercise could be. He started by taking short walks around his neighborhood every day. With each walk, he felt better. He kept making his walks longer and more challenging.

As John kept up with his walks, he noticed big changes in how he felt. He wasn't as sad, and he felt less worried. Moving his body helped him let go of stress and feel more relaxed.

Exercise also made John feel stronger inside. He started facing problems with more confidence. Exercise wasn't just something John did for his body; it was like his safe place, making him feel stronger and better about himself.

So, as you work on feeling better and happier, remember how good moving your body can be. Whether it's walking, working out, or doing yoga, find what you enjoy and do it often. Your body and mind will thank you.

PRIORITIZING SLEEP:

Sleep often gets overlooked, but it's super important for our overall health and well-being. Aim to get seven to nine hours of good-quality sleep each night. Establishing a relaxing bedtime routine can help you unwind and get ready for sleep.

Getting adequate sleep is crucial for various aspects of our health, including cognitive function, mood regulation, and immune function. Research shows that insufficient sleep can lead to increased stress, decreased productivity, and a higher risk of developing chronic conditions like obesity and heart disease.

Let's talk about why many of us struggle to get a good night's sleep. With the constant hustle and bustle of daily life, it's easy to prioritize other things over sleep. Stress, busy schedules, and technology can all interfere with our ability to wind down and get the rest we need. Many of us find ourselves lying awake at night, unable to quiet our minds and drift off to sleep.

Another common reason for sleep difficulties is poor sleep habits, such as irregular sleep schedules or consuming caffeine and heavy meals too close to bedtime. These habits can disrupt our body's natural sleep-wake cycle and make it harder to fall asleep and stay asleep.

Moreover, environmental factors like noise, light, and uncomfortable bedding can also impact sleep quality. For some, medical conditions such as sleep apnea, restless leg syndrome, or chronic pain can contribute to sleep disturbances.

Now, let's hear about Emily's experience. Emily used to struggle with insomnia and restless nights, tossing and turning until the early hours of the morning. But everything changed when she decided to make sleep a priority. Emily created a soothing bedtime ritual to help her wind down before bed. She would read a book, take a warm bath, and listen to calming music to relax her mind and body.

By making these changes and creating a peaceful sleep environment, Emily noticed a significant improvement in her sleep quality. She found herself falling asleep faster and staying asleep throughout the night. As a result, she woke up feeling refreshed and rejuvenated, ready to tackle whatever the day had in store.

So, what can you do if you're struggling to get a good night's sleep? Here are some solutions:

- Establish a consistent sleep schedule by going to bed and waking up at the same time every day, even on weekends.
- Create a relaxing bedtime routine to signal to your body that it's time to wind down. This could include activities like reading, taking a warm bath, listening to calming music, or deep breathing exercises.
- Make your sleep environment comfortable and conducive to sleep by keeping your bedroom cool, dark, and quiet.
- Limit exposure to screens and bright lights before bedtime, as they can interfere with your body's natural sleep-wake cycle.
- Avoid heavy meals, caffeine, and alcohol close to bedtime, as they can disrupt sleep.
- If stress or anxiety is keeping you awake at night, try relaxation techniques like deep breathing, meditation, or progressive muscle relaxation.

By implementing these strategies and making sleep a priority, you can improve your sleep quality and wake up feeling refreshed and rejuvenated, ready to tackle the day ahead. Just like Emily, you'll be able to overcome sleep struggles and enjoy the benefits of a good night's sleep.

Managing Stress:

Stress is a natural part of life, but too much of it can take a toll on your health and happiness. Finding healthy ways to manage stress is crucial for our overall well-being. You can try practicing mindfulness, engaging in hobbies you enjoy, or spending time in nature. It's important to prioritize self-care and set boundaries to protect your time and energy.

Let's dive into why managing stress is so important. Stress can affect both our physical and mental health, leading to issues like high blood pressure, anxiety, and depression. When we're constantly under stress, our bodies remain in a state of heightened alertness, which can have long-term consequences for our health.

In addition to work-related stress, there are other common sources of stress in our lives. Relationship conflicts, financial worries, and health concerns can all contribute to feelings of stress and overwhelm. It's essential to address these sources of stress and find healthy ways to cope.

Now, let's hear about Jamila's experience. Jamila experienced stress at work because she felt like she wasn't liked or accepted by her fellow workers and wasn't appreciated for her work effort. This made her feel undervalued and isolated, leading to increased stress and anxiety.

To address her work-related stress, Jamila decided to take proactive steps to improve her situation. She started by reaching out to her colleagues to build stronger relationships and foster a sense of camaraderie. She made an effort to communicate openly and assertively, expressing her concerns and seeking feedback on her work performance.

Additionally, Jamila sought support from her supervisor and HR department to address any underlying issues contributing to her stress. She advocated for herself and made it clear that she deserved to be treated with respect and appreciation for her contributions to the team.

As a result of her efforts, Jamila began to feel more supported and valued in the workplace. She noticed a positive shift in her relationships with her colleagues and felt more confident in her abilities. By taking proactive steps to address the root causes of her stress, Jamila was able to create a healthier and more fulfilling work environment for herself.

So, how can you manage stress in your own life? Here are some strategies to try:

Work-related Stress: Take proactive steps to address underlying issues contributing to your stress, such as communication problems or feelings of isolation. Reach out to colleagues, supervisors, or HR for support and feedback. Advocate for yourself and make it clear that you deserve to be treated with respect and appreciation for your work effort.

Relationship Conflicts: Communication is key when it comes to resolving conflicts in relationships. Try to express your feelings openly and listen to the other person's perspective with empathy and understanding. Consider seeking help from a therapist or counselor if you're having trouble resolving conflicts on your own.

Financial Worries: Take control of your finances by creating a budget and sticking to it. Identify areas where you can cut back on expenses and look for ways to increase your income, such as picking up a side gig or negotiating a raise. Remember to focus on what you can control and take proactive steps to improve your financial situation.

Health Concerns: Take care of your physical and mental health by prioritizing self-care activities like getting enough sleep, eating well, and staying physically active. Don't hesitate to reach out to healthcare professionals for support and guidance if you're dealing with health issues. Remember that it's okay to ask for help when you need it.

By incorporating these strategies into your daily routine, you can better manage stress and improve your overall well-being. Just like Jamila, you'll find yourself feeling more balanced, resilient, and capable of handling whatever life throws your way.

CULTIVATING HEALTHY HABITS:

Finally, let's focus on incorporating additional healthy habits into your routine to support your overall physical, mental, and social well-being. These habits, when combined with those we've already discussed, like managing stress, prioritizing sleep, exercising, and maintaining a healthy diet, can further enhance your quality of life.

Routine Check-ups: One important healthy habit to consider is scheduling regular medical check-ups with your healthcare provider. Routine check-ups can help monitor your health, detect any potential issues early, and provide valuable guidance for maintaining optimal well-being. By staying proactive about your healthcare, you can take control of your health and prevent future problems.

Daily Gratitude: One other important healthy habit to consider is practicing gratitude. Taking time each day to reflect on the things you're thankful for can improve your mood, reduce stress, and enhance your overall sense of well-being. Whether it's writing in a gratitude journal or simply expressing appreciation for the people and experiences in your life, exercising gratitude can have powerful effects on your mental and emotional health.

Nature Time: Another beneficial habit is spending time outdoors. Connecting with nature has been shown to reduce stress, improve mood, and boost cognitive function.

Whether you take a leisurely stroll in the park, go for a hike in the mountains, or simply sit outside and soak up the sunshine, spending time outdoors can have numerous benefits for your physical and mental well-being.

Mindful Living: Additionally, consider incorporating mindfulness practices into your daily routine. Mindfulness involves paying attention to the present moment with openness, curiosity, and acceptance. Practices like mindfulness meditation, deep breathing exercises, or mindful eating can help reduce stress, improve focus, and enhance overall well-being.

Social Connections: Social connections are also crucial for well-being. Spending time with friends and loved ones can provide emotional support, reduce feelings of loneliness, and increase feelings of happiness and belonging. Whether it's scheduling regular phone calls with friends, joining a club or community group, or volunteering in your local community, growing your social connections can have a positive impact on your mental and emotional health.

Creative Expression: Lastly, engaging in creative activities can be a great way to promote well-being. Whether it's painting, writing, gardening, or playing music, expressing yourself creatively can help reduce stress, boost mood, and foster a sense of fulfillment and purpose.

Now, let's hear about Carlos's journey to better health through healthy habits. Carlos used to neglect his health and avoid seeing his doctor regularly. But after experiencing a health scare where he felt chest pains and struggled to catch his breath, he realized the importance of taking care of himself. It was a wake-up call for him, and he knew he needed to make changes to prioritize his health and well-being.

Carlos started by scheduling regular check-ups with his doctor to monitor his health and catch any potential issues early. He also began practicing good hygiene habits like washing his hands regularly and taking extra precautions to prevent illness.

By prioritizing his health and well-being, Carlos noticed significant improvements in his energy levels, mood, and overall quality of life. He felt more empowered and in control of his health, and he was grateful for the opportunity to make positive changes in his life.

By incorporating these additional healthy habits into your daily life, you can further enhance your overall well-being and happiness. Remember, small changes can lead to significant improvements in your physical, mental, and social well-being over time. So, embrace these healthy living habits, and watch as they empower you to live your best life, filled with vitality, energy, and joy.

In a Nutshell:

In this bonus chapter on healthy living, we've covered the basics of living well to stay healthy and happy. It's about more than just dodging sickness—it's about building habits that support your body, mind, and heart, keeping you feeling good for the long haul.

We've talked about eating right, moving your body in ways you enjoy, getting enough sleep, and managing stress. Plus, we've highlighted the importance of regular check-ups, gratitude, time outdoors, mindfulness, social connections, and creative activities. These habits aren't just good for your health—they're good for your overall well-being. Keep it up!

Continuing Education Resources for Healthy Living:

1. *How Not to Die: Discover the Foods Scientifically Proven to Prevent and Reverse Disease* by Michael Greger, MD
2. *Eat, Move, Sleep: How Small Choices Lead to Big Changes* by Tom Rath
3. *The Relaxation Response* by Herbert Benson
4. *Why We Sleep: Unlocking the Power of Sleep and Dreams* by Matthew Walker
5. *The Blue Zones: Lessons for Living Longer From the People Who've Lived the Longest* by Dan Buettner

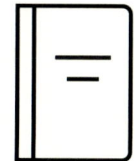

JOURNALING PROMPTS FOR HEALTHY LIVING:

Journaling prompts are a great way to help you engage with the material and reflect on your own experiences. Here are two prompts for this chapter:

Journal Prompt 1: Reflect on your current habits related to healthy living, including nutrition, exercise, sleep, stress management, and self-care. Are there areas where you feel you could make improvements? What specific actions could you take to enhance your overall well-being in these areas? Consider setting realistic goals for yourself and creating a plan to implement healthy habits into your daily routine.

Journal Prompt 2: Think about a time when you made a positive change to support your health and well-being. What motivated you to make this change, and how did it impact your life? Reflect on any challenges you faced along the way and how you overcame them. Write about the lessons you learned from this experience and how you can apply them to other areas of your life where you want to prioritize healthy living.

BONUS 2:
ACHIEVING FINANCIAL WELLNESS

"You must gain control over your money, or the lack of it will forever control you."

- DAVE RAMSEY

Financial wellness: It's about checking how good you are at handling your money. Getting better at it means doing smarter things with your cash, like setting goals and working to reach them. The big goal? To make your life better overall.

***

Ever find yourself juggling bills like a circus performer without a safety net? Don't worry, you're not alone. In this chapter, we're going to break down the importance of managing your money wisely and provide you with practical tips to help you navigate the wild waters of personal finance. Get ready to discover the tools and strategies you need to take control of your financial future and live your best financial life.

THE LINK BETWEEN MONEY AND HAPPINESS:

The connection between money and happiness is a common question, but the answer isn't simple. A common finding in psychological and sociological research shows that feeling secure financially is linked to feeling satisfied with life overall. When you're not worried about money, you can focus on what's really important—like spending time with loved ones and doing things you enjoy.

But it's not just about having a lot of money; it's also about how you use it. Many people find that true happiness doesn't come from buying expensive things but from having meaningful experiences. By choosing experiences over stuff, people often feel more fulfilled and content in their lives.

THE IMPORTANCE OF MANAGING YOUR MONEY WISELY:

Think Managing your money or finances is another important tool for our life skill toolbox. Think of your finances like a toolbox that helps you navigate life's twists and turns. When you have control over your money, you're better equipped to handle unexpected challenges and pursue your goals with confidence. It's not just about budgeting and saving—it's about creating a foundation for financial security and freedom.

By effectively managing your money, you can reduce stress and worry, allowing you to focus on what truly matters in life. Whether it's pursuing your passions, supporting your loved ones, or planning for the future, financial stability provides a sense of peace and security.

Furthermore, making smart financial decisions can lead to long-term benefits, such as building wealth, achieving financial independence, and creating opportunities for yourself and your family. By investing in your financial wellness, you're investing in your future happiness and success.

So, as you embark on your journey toward financial wellness, remember that every dollar you save and every smart choice you make brings you closer to a brighter, more secure future. With the right knowledge and mindset, you can navigate the waters of financial management with confidence and clarity, ensuring a smoother journey toward your goals.

UNDERSTANDING FINANCIAL WELLNESS:

Imagine yourself aboard a sturdy ship, sailing across a vast and stormy sea. In the distance, a tall lighthouse stands strong, its light shining bright and showing the way through the dark waves. This lighthouse is like your financial wellness—it helps you stay steady and find your path through the ups and downs of managing your money.

Just like how a lighthouse guides ships safely to shore, financial wellness helps you navigate life's challenges and make smart decisions with your money. It gives you the tools you need to weather tough times, adapt to changes, and steer toward a brighter future.

So, as you sail on your journey toward financial wellness, let the light of knowledge and good choices guide your way. Welcome the adventure of managing your money, knowing that each step forward brings you closer to a life full of abundance and fulfillment.

In the following sections, we'll discuss earning, savings, investing, spending, and accumulating assets and how they all relate to achieving your financial wellness.

EARNING: MAXIMIZE YOUR INCOME POTENTIAL

Earning money is the foundation of your financial journey—it's what fuels your ability to save, invest, and achieve your financial goals. Whether you're employed full-time, freelancing, or running your own business, there are various strategies you can employ to maximize your income potential and bolster your financial wellness.

Enhance Your Skills and Education: Investing in your skills and education can significantly boost your earning potential. Consider pursuing additional certifications, attending workshops or seminars, or enrolling in further education programs related to your field. By continuously upgrading your skill set, you can position yourself for higher-paying job opportunities and career advancement.

Negotiate Your Salary: Don't be afraid to advocate for yourself when it comes to your salary. Research industry standards and salary ranges for your position and use this information to negotiate a higher salary during job interviews or performance reviews. Highlight your accomplishments, skills, and value to the company to justify your request for a higher compensation package.

Explore Side Hustle Opportunities: In addition to your primary source of income, consider exploring side hustle opportunities to supplement your earnings. This could involve leveraging your existing skills and interests to offer freelance services, consulting, or selling products online. Starting a side hustle not only provides an additional income stream but also offers flexibility and autonomy in how you earn money.

Monetize Your Passion Projects: If you have a hobby or passion project that you enjoy, consider monetizing it to generate extra income. This could involve selling handmade crafts, offering online courses or workshops, or monetizing a blog or YouTube channel. By leveraging your passions and talents, you can turn your hobbies into lucrative income streams that contribute to your overall financial well-being.

Invest in Income-generating Assets: Explore opportunities to invest in income-generating assets that can supplement your primary source of income. This could include rental properties, dividend-paying stocks, peer-to-peer lending platforms, or royalties from intellectual property. By diversifying your income sources, you can create multiple streams of revenue that provide stability and resilience against economic fluctuations.

By implementing these strategies to maximize your income potential, you can increase your earning capacity and accelerate your journey toward financial wellness. Whether through advancing your career, exploring side hustles, or investing in income-generating assets, taking proactive steps to boost your income lays the groundwork for a more secure and prosperous financial future. Remember, these are just a few opportunities for generating additional income, and there are many other strategies you can explore to enhance your financial well-being.

SAVINGS: BUILD YOUR FINANCIAL SAFETY NET

Having a robust savings account is akin to having a safety net—it provides a cushion to soften the impact of unexpected financial challenges. It gives you peace of mind knowing that you have funds readily available when needed.

Set Clear Savings Goals: Begin by identifying specific savings goals that align with your financial priorities and aspirations. Whether it's creating an emergency fund to cover unexpected expenses, saving for a dream vacation, or setting aside funds for a major purchase like a home or car, having clear objectives can help you stay motivated and focused on building your savings.

Automate Your Savings: One of the most effective ways to grow your savings effortlessly is by automating your savings process. Set up recurring transfers from your checking account to your savings account on a regular basis, such as each paycheck or monthly. Automating your savings ensures that a portion of your income is consistently allocated toward your savings goals without requiring constant manual intervention.

Trim Expenses and Redirect Savings: Take a close look at your monthly expenses and identify areas where you can cut back or eliminate unnecessary spending. This could involve reducing discretionary expenses such as dining out, entertainment, or subscription services and reallocating those savings toward your savings goals. Small adjustments to your spending habits can add up over time and accelerate your progress in building a substantial financial safety net.

Establish an Emergency Fund: One of the most critical components of a financial safety net is an emergency fund. Aim to set aside enough funds to cover essential living expenses for three to six months in case of unforeseen circumstances such as job loss, medical emergencies, or major home or car repairs. Having an emergency fund provides you with financial security and peace of mind, knowing that you have a financial buffer to rely on during times of crisis.

Consider High-yield Savings Accounts or Other Investment Vehicles: Explore options to maximize the growth potential of your savings by parking your funds in high-yield savings accounts or other investment vehicles that offer competitive interest rates or potential returns. While traditional savings accounts provide a safe and accessible option for storing your emergency fund and short-term savings, exploring alternative investment options can help your savings grow more efficiently over the long term.

By implementing these strategies to build your financial safety net, you can strengthen your financial resilience and prepare yourself for whatever life may throw your way. Whether through automated savings, expense trimming, or establishing an emergency fund, prioritizing savings as part of your financial strategy sets the foundation for a more secure and prosperous future, providing not only financial stability but also peace of mind and reducing stress and anxiety.

INVESTING: GROW YOUR WEALTH OVER TIME

Investing is like planting seeds for your financial future. It's about making your money work for you to grow wealth over time. By putting your money into investments that match your goals and comfort level with risk, you can create opportunities for passive income, keep up with rising prices, and build up savings for retirement or other big expenses. Investing helps you take charge of your financial destiny, spread out where your money comes from, and move toward long-term security and calm about money matters.

Understand your Investment Options: Before diving into the world of investing, it's essential to familiarize yourself with the various investment options available to you. Consider factors such as your risk tolerance, time horizon, and financial goals when evaluating different investment opportunities. Common investment vehicles include stocks, bonds, mutual funds, real estate, and retirement accounts like 401(k)s and IRAs.

Educate Yourself: Investing can seem daunting, especially if you're new to the game. Take the time to educate yourself about the fundamentals of investing, including concepts like asset allocation, diversification, and risk management. There are numerous resources available, such as books, online courses, and educational websites, that can help you build a solid foundation of investment knowledge. I have listed a few recommendations at the end of this chapter.

Seek Professional Guidance: If you're unsure where to begin or feel overwhelmed by the complexities of investing, consider seeking guidance from a financial advisor. A qualified advisor can help you assess your financial situation, define your investment objectives, and develop a personalized investment strategy tailored to your needs and preferences. They can also provide valuable insights and recommendations to help you navigate the investment landscape with confidence.

Start Small and Stay Consistent: If you're new to investing, it's okay to start small and gradually increase your investment contributions over time. Consider setting up automatic contributions to your investment accounts, such as a brokerage account or retirement plan, to ensure consistent and disciplined investing. By investing regularly, you can take advantage of dollar-cost averaging—buying securities at regular intervals, regardless of market conditions—to potentially lower your average cost per share over time and benefit from the power of compounding.

Monitor and Adjust Your Portfolio: As you initiate your investment journey, regularly monitor the performance of your investment portfolio and make adjustments as needed. Keep an eye on market trends, economic indicators, and changes in your financial situation that may warrant modifications to your investment strategy.

However, be cautious of making frequent adjustments, as attempting to time the market can be risky and may lead to suboptimal returns. Instead, consider adopting a buy-and-hold strategy, where you invest in quality assets with the intention of holding them for the long term, regardless of short-term market fluctuations. Over time, this approach can help you avoid the pitfalls of emotional decision-making and capitalize on the long-term growth potential of the market.

By embracing investing as a means to grow your wealth over time, you can take proactive steps toward achieving your financial aspirations and building a more secure future for yourself and your loved ones. Whether through stocks, bonds, mutual funds, or retirement accounts, investing offers the opportunity to harness the power of compounding and achieve financial success in the long run.

SPENDING: CREATE HEALTHY MONEY HABITS

Spending money wisely is a crucial part of managing your finances effectively. Just like earning and saving, how you spend your money plays a significant role in your overall financial well-being. By adopting mindful spending habits and prioritizing your expenses, you can make the most of your hard-earned money and work toward achieving your financial goals.

Create and Stick to a Budget: A budget serves as a roadmap for your finances, helping you allocate your income toward essential expenses, savings, and discretionary spending. Start by tracking your expenses to gain a clear understanding of where your money is going each month. Identify areas where you can cut back or eliminate unnecessary spending and allocate those savings to your financial priorities. By sticking to a budget, you can ensure that your spending aligns with your financial goals and prevents you from overspending.

Practice Mindful Spending: Mindful spending involves making intentional and thoughtful choices about how you use your money. Before making a purchase, ask yourself whether it aligns with your values and priorities. Consider whether the item or experience will bring you long-term satisfaction and fulfillment or if it's merely a fleeting indulgence. By being mindful of your spending decisions, you can avoid impulse purchases and focus your resources on what truly matters to you.

Seek Ways to Save: Look for opportunities to save money on everyday expenses without sacrificing quality of life. This could involve shopping sales, using coupons, or taking advantage of rewards programs to stretch your dollars further. Additionally, consider adopting frugal habits such as cooking meals at home, carpooling, or using public transportation to reduce your monthly expenses. Small changes in your spending habits can add up over time and contribute to significant savings.

Prioritize Your Spending: When allocating your financial resources, prioritize spending on items and experiences that bring you genuine joy, fulfillment, and value. Focus on the things that enhance your quality of life and align with your long-term goals while cutting back on non-essential or frivolous purchases. By consciously directing your spending to what matters most to you, you can live within your means and achieve a greater sense of financial security and contentment.

By incorporating these strategies into your spending habits, you can cultivate a healthier relationship with money and move closer to your financial aspirations. Whether through budgeting, mindful spending, or seeking ways to save, adopting smart spending habits empowers you to make the most of your financial resources and build a more secure and fulfilling future.

ACCUMULATE ASSETS: BUILD LONG-TERM WEALTH

Building long-term wealth involves strategically accumulating assets that appreciate in value over time, providing you with financial security and opportunities for growth. While traditional investments like stocks and real estate are commonly used to build wealth, exploring alternative asset classes and passive income opportunities can further enhance your financial resilience and prosperity.

Explore Alternative Asset Classes: In addition to conventional investments, consider diversifying your portfolio by exploring alternative asset classes that offer unique opportunities for growth. Alternative investments such as cryptocurrency, peer-to-peer lending, or collectibles like art and rare coins can provide diversification benefits and potentially higher returns than traditional asset classes. However, it's essential to start slow when investing in areas you are just learning about. Conduct thorough research and understand the risks associated with these investments before committing your funds.

Seek Opportunities for Passive Income: Passive income streams, which are earnings generated with minimal ongoing effort or active involvement once established, can serve as a valuable source of ongoing revenue, supplementing your primary income and accelerating your wealth-building efforts.

While it may require some initial effort to set up passive income streams, such as rental properties, dividend-paying stocks, or royalties from intellectual property, they can eventually provide a more sustainable source of wealth over the long term with less ongoing work compared to active income sources.

By investing time and resources upfront, you can unlock financial freedom and create a more secure financial future.

Embrace Diversification: Diversifying your investment portfolio is key to managing risk and maximizing returns. Instead of putting all your eggs in one basket, spread your investments across a range of asset classes and investment vehicles. By diversifying your portfolio, you can mitigate the impact of market fluctuations and increase the likelihood of achieving consistent returns over time.

Remember to periodically review and rebalance your portfolio to ensure it remains aligned with your financial goals and risk tolerance.

Consider Long-term Growth Opportunities: When evaluating potential investments, focus on assets with the potential for long-term growth and appreciation. Look for opportunities to invest in industries and sectors poised for future growth, such as technology, renewable energy, or emerging markets. By taking a long-term perspective and investing in assets with strong growth prospects, you can position yourself to capitalize on market trends and build wealth steadily over time.

By accumulating assets strategically and diversifying your investment portfolio, you can create a robust foundation for long-term wealth accumulation and financial success. Whether through traditional investments, alternative asset classes, or passive income strategies, exploring diverse wealth-building opportunities empowers you to achieve your financial goals and secure a brighter future for yourself and your loved ones.

Moreover, enhancing your financial well-being in this way can contribute to greater overall life satisfaction and provide you with the resources needed to thrive in all aspects of your life.

PROTECT YOUR FINANCIAL FUTURE: INSURANCE AND ESTATE PLANNING

Safeguarding your financial future is a critical aspect of comprehensive financial planning. By securing adequate insurance coverage and implementing effective estate planning strategies, you can protect your assets, mitigate risks, and ensure the well-being of your loved ones both now and in the future.

Evaluate Your Insurance Needs: Insurance serves as a crucial safety net, providing financial protection against unforeseen events and emergencies. Regularly review your insurance policies to assess whether you have the appropriate coverage for your current circumstances.

Consider factors such as health, disability, life, auto, and homeowners' insurance to ensure comprehensive protection against life's uncertainties. By maintaining adequate insurance coverage, you can safeguard your financial stability and avoid potentially devastating financial losses in the event of an unexpected crisis.

Plan For Life's Transitions: Estate planning is a vital component of protecting your financial legacy and ensuring your wishes are carried out effectively. Take the time to create a comprehensive estate plan that addresses key aspects such as wills, trusts, and powers of attorney.

Designate beneficiaries for your assets, establish guardianship arrangements for minor children, and outline your preferences for medical care and end-of-life decisions. By proactively planning for life's transitions, you can provide clarity and guidance to your loved ones during challenging times and minimize the potential for family conflicts or disputes.

Seek Professional Guidance: Navigating the complexities of insurance and estate planning can be daunting, especially if you're unfamiliar with legal or financial terminology. Consider seeking guidance from qualified professionals such as insurance agents, estate planning attorneys, or financial advisors who can provide personalized advice tailored to your specific needs and objectives.

These experts can help you identify potential gaps in your insurance coverage, navigate the intricacies of estate planning laws, and develop a customized plan that aligns with your goals and values.

Regularly Review and Update: Life is constantly changing, and so are your financial circumstances. Regularly review and update your insurance policies and estate plan to reflect any significant life events or changes in your financial situation. Whether it's getting married, having children, buying a home, or experiencing a change in employment, these life transitions may necessitate adjustments to your insurance coverage and estate planning documents.

By staying proactive and vigilant, you can ensure that your financial affairs remain current and relevant to your evolving needs and priorities.

By prioritizing insurance coverage and estate planning, you can protect your financial well-being and provide security and stability for yourself and your loved ones over the long term. Whether it's shielding against unexpected risks or planning for the future, taking proactive steps to safeguard your financial future offers peace of mind and confidence in your ability to weather life's uncertainties with resilience and strength.

In a Nutshell:

Financial wellness isn't solely about the size of your bank account; it's about developing smart money habits that pave the way for lasting security and tranquility. By focusing on earning, saving, investing, spending, accumulating assets, and safeguarding your financial future through insurance and estate planning, you're not only building a sturdy financial foundation but also positioning yourself to flourish in every facet of life. So, embrace these principles, take charge of your financial journey, and watch as you rise and thrive toward a brighter, more prosperous future.

CONTINUING EDUCATION RESOURCES FOR ACHIEVING FINANCIAL WELLNESS:

1. *The Total Money Makeover: A Proven Plan for Financial Fitness* by Dave Ramsey
2. *Rich Dad Poor Dad: What the Rich Teach Their Kids About Money That the Poor and Middle Class Do Not!* by Robert T. Kiyosaki
3. *The Millionaire Next Door: The Surprising Secrets of America's Wealthy* by Thomas J. Stanley and William D. Danko
4. *Your Money or Your Life: 9 Steps to Transforming Your Relationship with Money and Achieving Financial Independence* by Vicki Robin and Joe Dominguez
5. *The Simple Path to Wealth: Your Road Map to Financial Independence and a Rich, Free Life* by J.L. Collins

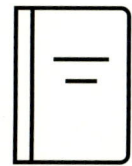

JOURNALING PROMPTS FOR ACHIEVING FINANCIAL WELLNESS:

Journaling prompts are a great way to help you engage with the material and reflect on your own experiences. Here are two prompts for this chapter:

Journal Prompt 1: Reflect on a time when you felt financially stressed or uncertain about your financial future. What were the circumstances that led to these feelings, and how did you cope with them? Were there any specific strategies or tools you used to navigate through the challenges? What did you learn from that experience, and how has it influenced your approach to managing your finances since then? Consider how improving your financial wellness could have helped alleviate some of the stress or uncertainty you felt during that time.

Journal Prompt 2: Imagine yourself five years from now, living your best financial life. What does that look like to you? Describe the financial goals you've achieved, the habits you've cultivated, and the sense of security and fulfillment you experience as a result. How has improving your financial wellness positively impacted other areas of your life, such as your relationships, career, or personal well-being? What steps can you take today to move closer to that vision of your future self? Reflect on the journey toward financial wellness as an ongoing adventure, filled with opportunities for growth, resilience, and abundance.

EPILOGUE:

Now that you've worked your way through "Small Changes BIG RESULTS," plus the two bonus chapters, it's time for you to reflect: What will you do with the wisdom you've gained? How will you move forward and live a more fulfilling life?

The power is in your hands. You hold the keys to unlock a future brimming with purpose, joy, and possibility. It starts with taking action on these small changes, one step at a time.

First, reflect on the insights you've discovered and the strategies you've learned. Consider how you can integrate them into your daily life, starting today. Whether it's cultivating gratitude, practicing kindness, or setting meaningful goals, each small step contributes to your journey of growth and fulfillment.

Next, surround yourself with support. Share your aspirations with friends, family, or a supportive community. Seek out mentors, role models, or like-minded individuals who can inspire and encourage you along the way.

Finally, embrace the adventure ahead with courage and enthusiasm. Embrace the challenges as opportunities for growth. Celebrate your successes, no matter how small. And remember, you're not alone on this journey. Together, we can rise above obstacles and create a life that truly brings us joy and satisfaction.

So, what will you do next? How will you improve your life in your own unique way? The choice is yours. Seize the moment, embrace the possibilities, and begin the amazing journey that beckons. Your best life is ready to be lived.

ACKNOWLEDGEMENTS:

In the journey of bringing this book to life, there have been many hands on deck, each contributing in their own unique way.

To my wife, Joyce, who deserves a special mention for her unwavering support and understanding during the early mornings and long afternoons of writing. Your patience and encouragement were the bedrock upon which this book was built.

To my friends, relatives, and colleagues in both behavioral health pharmacy and writing, thank you for your camaraderie, feedback, and for lending an ear when I needed to bounce ideas around.

A heartfelt thank you to the experts and professionals from both Fiverr and Reedsy, for their expertise, guidance, and knowledge who have enriched and shaped this manuscript into its final form. Thank you, Haley and Goran.

Gratitude also goes out to the unsung heroes—the baristas, delivery drivers, and anyone who kept me caffeinated and supplied during those marathon writing sessions. Your support ensured I had everything I needed to stay focused on bringing this book to fruition without interruption

And, most importantly, to the readers: thank you for your interest in the topic of personal growth and for considering the ideas presented within these pages. May they serve as catalysts for positive changes, illustrating how small adjustments can lead to significant transformations in your lives.

ABOUT THE AUTHOR:

Hey there, I'm Jay. I've been fortunate to receive awards for my writing, blogging, and work as a behavioral health pharmacist. Wondering if you're truly happy with your life? That's where I come in. My goal is to educate, inspire, and empower you to overcome obstacles and chase your dreams. Through my writing, I aim to help you live with purpose and intention, drawing from my personal growth journey and insights from personal development experts.

Based in the University Circle area of Cleveland, Ohio, I explore the essence of purpose-driven living. Armed with degrees from The Ohio State University and Texas A&M University-Corpus Christi, I bring a unique blend of expertise to my work. My passion lies in guiding individuals to discover and embrace their life's purpose, as showcased in my book, "Rise Above the Rut." Rooted in a genuine desire to help others, I introduce my proprietary 3-Step Process, a cornerstone of my mission.

Outside of writing, I routinely donate my time to volunteer for the Association for Continuing Education (ACE) at Case Western Reserve University. One of our main projects is the annual Book Sale, which has evolved from a simple book exchange into one of the region's largest sales, drawing dealers and collectors from neighboring states. Proceeds from the sale support ACE programs and fund our annual contribution to Off-Campus Studies. It's a fulfilling way to blend my love for education with community involvement.

When I'm not writing, reading, working, or volunteering, you'll find me enjoying the harmonies of Severance Hall with the Cleveland Orchestra or exploring the vibrant art scene at the Cleveland Museum of Art with my partner, Joyce. As a lifelong learner, I seek wisdom at the Chautauqua Institution in New York, reflecting my dedication to personal growth. I also enjoy learning opportunities at OLLI - The Osher Lifelong Learning Institute (OLLI) at Eckerd College offers curious adults life-enriching courses, lectures, excursions, and experiences, all focused on complimenting an individual's journey to learn about, engage with, and contribute to the world around them.

My life is a rich tapestry woven with various interests and passions. Beyond my professional endeavors, I find joy in reading, indulging in smooth jazz, and rocking out to classic tunes. I also relish the experience of watching a good movie, attending a captivating play, or taking a mindful walk. This symphony of interests and pursuits aligns with my motto to "live with intention, express gratitude, uplift others, and stand by my commitments," guiding me in both personal and professional spheres.

Ready to embark on a journey of purposeful living? Connect with me on my Facebook Author Page (Jay Nesbit Author) or explore more on my website, www.jaynesbit.com. Let's make this journey together. "Never give up living your dream."

CAN YOU DO ME TWO QUICK FAVORS?

First off, big thanks for snagging a copy of this book. It's truly awesome to know you're diving into these pages.

I poured my heart and soul into researching and writing this book. Then came the editing process, working with a designer to nail down that killer cover, and finally, launching it out into the world.

I'm hoping this book becomes your trusty sidekick on your journey to a better life. And hey, let's make a pact right now: promise me you'll never, ever give up on chasing your dreams. Deal?

Now, I've got a couple of quick favors to ask: could you spare a few minutes to drop a review on Goodreads, Amazon, or wherever you bought the book? Your thoughts and feedback mean the world to me. Seriously, every review is like a little burst of sunshine in my day.

And here's the thing about reviews: they're not just for me. They're for all those folks out there who are on the hunt for a book just like this one to help them level up their lives. Your honest review could be the guiding light they need.

Plus, while you're at it, would you mind joining my mailing list on my website www.jaynesbit.com? You'll get my twice-monthly blogs filled with more life-changing words delivered straight to your inbox. It's a win-win!

Your support and feedback help me grow as a writer. I read each and every review and soak up all the wisdom and insight you've got to offer. So yeah, your words? They're kind of a big deal.

Thanks again for being awesome and joining me on this adventure. Let's make some magic happen, shall we? ✹

UNLOCK YOUR TRUE POTENTIAL

RISE ABOVE THE RUT

REDISCOVERING JOY AND
PURPOSE IN YOUR LIFE

JAY NESBIT

Jay Nesbit's "Rise Above the Rut" introduces a transformative 3-step process that serves as a bridge, taking you from your current state of meaningless monotony to a more fulfilling life. From uncovering your unique purpose to writing an action plan and achieving relentless progress, Jay Nesbit's game-changing book is ideal for those seeking guidance in our fast-paced, unforgiving society.

This book is a must-read for those seeking a more meaningful and satisfying existence, offering practical steps to turn dreams into reality. Whether you're in a rut or simply want to achieve greater self-satisfaction and happiness, "Rise Above the Rut" is a valuable companion on your journey.

-   THE INTERNATIONAL REVIEW OF BOOKS

Another meaningful book in Jay Nesbit's **Living with Purpose Series**

Made in United States
North Haven, CT
02 March 2025

66407113R00164